W9-DGJ-978

Alexander Graham Bell

Making Connections

Owen Gingerich
General Editor

Alexander Graham Bell

Making Connections

Naomi Pasachoff

Oxford University Press
New York • Oxford

JB
BelA
c.1

To my daughters, Eloise and Deborah, whose birth dates coincide with anniversaries of crucial events in the life of Alexander Graham Bell: Eloise ("Here's the thing: I'm always on the telephone"), February 27, 1975, a century after the formation of the Bell Patent Association; and Deborah, May 8, 1977, 99 years after the birth of Bell's older daughter, Elsie.

Oxford University Press

Oxford   New York
Athens Auckland Bangkok Bogotá Bombay
Buenos Aires Calcutta Cape Town Dar es Salaam
Delhi Florence Hong Kong Istanbul Karachi
Kuala Lumpur Madras Madrid Melbourne
Mexico City Nairobi Paris Singapore
Taipei Tokyo Toronto
and associated companies in
Berlin   Ibadan

Copyright © 1996 by Naomi Pasachoff
Published by Oxford University Press, Inc.,
198 Madison Avenue, New York, New York 10016

Oxford is a registered trademark of Oxford University Press

Design: Design Oasis
Layout: Loraine Machlin
Picture research: Laura Kreiss

Library of Congress Cataloging-in-Publication Data

Pasachoff, Naomi E.
Alexander Graham Bell / Naomi Pasachoff
p. cm. — (Oxford Portraits in Science)
Includes bibliographical references and index.
ISBN 0-19-509908-7 (library edition)
1. Bell, Alexander Graham, 1847-1822—Juvenile literature. 2. Inventors—United
States—Biography—Juvenile literature. [1. Bell, Alexander Graham, 1847-1922.
2. Inventors.] I. Title. II. Series.
TK6143.B4P38   1996
621.385'092—dc20   95-45024
                               CIP

9 8 7 6 5 4 3 2 1
Printed in the United States of America
on acid-free paper

On the cover: *A portrait of Alexander Graham Bell from 1871;* Inset: *Bell making the first telephone call between New York and Chicago in 1892.*
Frontispiece: *Bell descends the stairs of his tetrahedral tower, 1907.*

Contents

Chapter 1. "A Preparation for Scientific Work" 8

    Sidebar: Electromagnetism: The Scientific
    Principle Underlying the Telephone 20

Chapter 2. "Great Discoveries and Inventions. . .
    Arise from the Observation of Little Things" 24

    Sidebar: Sound, Speech, and Hearing 30

Chapter 3. "Onward Irresistibly in the Direction of the
    Telephone" 40

    Sidebar: How a Telephone Works 56

Chapter 4. "A Target for the World to Shoot At" 61

Chapter 5. "Science. . .The Highest of All Things" 76

    Sidebar: The "Photophone," Fiber Optics,
    and Wireless Telephones 84

Chapter 6. "My Life Work. . .
    The Teaching of Speech to the Deaf" 91

Chapter 7. "The Age of the Flying Machine
    Was at Hand" 105

Chapter 8. "I Want Many More Years of Life
    to Finish It All" 118

Chronology 133

Further Reading 136

Index 139

The titles of each of this book's chapters are quotations from Alexander Graham Bell. Bell's lengthy association with the National Geographic Society is reflected in several chapter titles. Chapters 1, 3, and 6 are quotations from Bell's article "Prehistoric Telephone Days," which appeared in the March 1922 issue of *National Geographic Magazine*. The titles of chapters 2 and 7 also come from articles Bell wrote for *National Geographic,* the former from "Discovery and Invention," which appeared in the June 1914 issue, and the latter from "Aerial Locomotion," which appeared in the January 1907 issue.

Bell's devotion to his wife, Mabel, is reflected in the remaining three chapter titles. The titles of chapters 4 and 8 come from letters Bell wrote to Mabel dated September 9, 1878, and February 8, 1885, respectively. Chapter 5 takes its title from a remark of Bell's quoted in Mabel's diary entry for March 8, 1879.

As *Alexander Graham Bell: Making Connections* neared completion, an unexpected connection linking my own spouse to Alexander Graham Bell and the National Geographic Society came to my attention. My husband, Jay M. Pasachoff, is an astronomer, one of whose research specialties is solar eclipses. For over two decades his research has been partly supported by the National Geographic Committee on Research and Exploration. In the April 1996 issue of *National Geographic Magazine,* in an article describing the work of the committee, my husband's picture performing an experiment at a recent eclipse appears with this caption: "Beginning with Alexander Graham Bell's coverage of a 1900 eclipse, the Society has sponsored space studies ranging from the analysis of tiny asteroids to all-sky surveys."

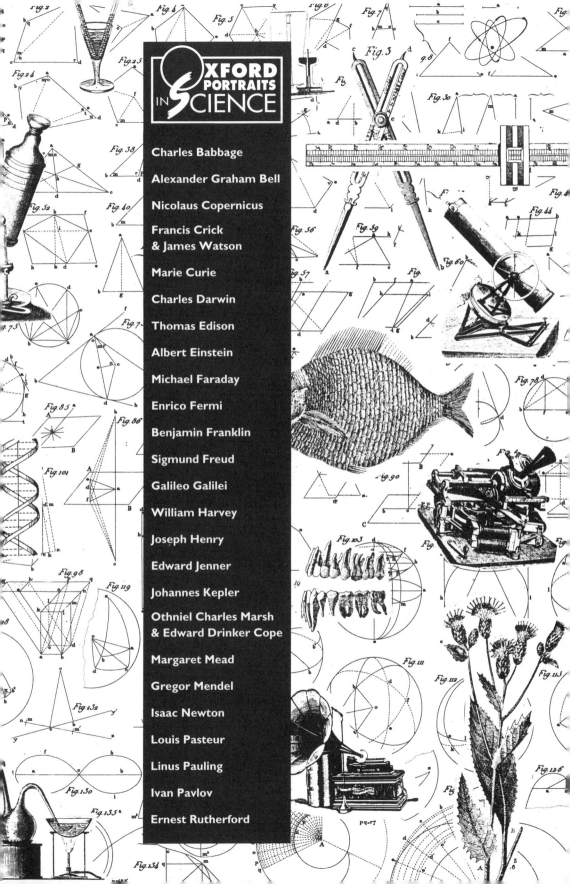

OXFORD PORTRAITS IN SCIENCE

Charles Babbage

Alexander Graham Bell

Nicolaus Copernicus

Francis Crick
& James Watson

Marie Curie

Charles Darwin

Thomas Edison

Albert Einstein

Michael Faraday

Enrico Fermi

Benjamin Franklin

Sigmund Freud

Galileo Galilei

William Harvey

Joseph Henry

Edward Jenner

Johannes Kepler

Othniel Charles Marsh
& Edward Drinker Cope

Margaret Mead

Gregor Mendel

Isaac Newton

Louis Pasteur

Linus Pauling

Ivan Pavlov

Ernest Rutherford

"A Preparation for Scientific Work"

The thin, black-haired, whiskered young man, two days shy of his 28th birthday, felt uncomfortable. It was not the bitter cold of this March day in Washington, D.C., that underlay his mood. He, an aspiring inventor, was in the office of 78-year-old Joseph Henry, the secretary of the Smithsonian Institution. Henry was one of the best-known physicists in the country and an expert in the still-young science of electricity. The Smithsonian, only a year older than the young inventor, had been established by the United States Congress in 1846 as a nonprofit research institution, and it was the job of its secretary to direct its activities. The young man waiting in his office had traveled from Boston to Washington, where he planned to file a patent at the Patent Office on an invention he was trying to perfect, the "harmonic telegraph." He hoped his invention would be capable, when perfected, of sending many telegraph messages at a single time. As he described his ideas, however, he could sense the old man's lack of excitement.

Then the young man mentioned an electrical effect he had noted in his work. When he passed electrical current through a spiral of insulated copper wire and interrupted

Alexander Graham Bell in 1871, at the age of 24, when he was appointed professor of vocal physiology at Boston University's School of Oratory.

the current at intervals, he heard a noise come from the spiral. The effect had not seemed particularly significant to him, but all of a sudden Henry sat up attentively. He asked Alexander Graham Bell—for that was the name on the Bostonian's business card—for permission to repeat the experiment. Henry would publish the results through the Smithsonian and would be sure to name Bell as the source. Bell told Henry he would be delighted, adding that he happened to have the apparatus with him in Washington.

Although the weather was nasty and Henry was obviously suffering from a cold, the old man got up to get his coat, order his carriage, and proceed directly to Bell's rooms. Worried about Henry's health, however, Bell volunteered to return the next day at noon with the instruments.

Thus, on March 2, 1875, Alexander Graham Bell and Joseph Henry together observed with mutual enthusiasm the sound produced by passing an electric current through an insulated spiral of copper wire. Relaxed now in the august scientist's company, Bell decided to consult him about another project he was working on—an instrument to send the human voice over a telegraph wire. After describing in some detail the concepts underlying the project, Bell admitted that he lacked sufficient background in electricity. Many problems remained to be solved before his theory could be transformed into functioning equipment. He asked Henry's advice: Should he tackle the problems himself, or publish the idea and leave it to others more proficient in electrical science to achieve the breakthrough?

As Bell later wrote his parents, Henry made two encouraging remarks. He told Bell, "You have the germ of a great invention. Work at it." Then, without mincing words, the old man stressed that if lack of electrical experience was holding Bell back, "Get it!"

In the same letter Bell confided to his parents, "I cannot tell you how much these two words have encouraged me. . . . Such a chimerical idea as telegraphing vocal sounds would indeed to most minds seem scarcely feasible enough to spend time working over." Years later he said, "But for Joseph Henry I should never have gone on with the telephone."

That two-day encounter in March 1875 inspired Alexander Graham Bell to pursue his interest in the instrument we now know as the telephone, and the world has never been the same since.

It is not really surprising that Bell was fascinated by the idea of an instrument for conveying speech. He was the son and grandson of men whose professional lives also revolved around speech and communication. His grandfather, Alexander Bell (1790–1865), began his career as a shoemaker and an actor in Scotland. He later became a "corrector of defective utterance" (what we would call a speech therapist) in London, and was thus the first Bell to specialize in speech production and sound. One of his sons, Alexander Melville Bell (1819–1905)—called Melville, to distinguish him from his father—was his father's professional assistant. When Melville fell in love with and married Eliza Grace Symonds of Edinburgh, he established in the Scottish capital a practice modeled on his father's. Melville and Eliza soon had sons of their own: Melville (born in 1845 and nicknamed Melly), Alexander (born in 1847 and nicknamed Aleck), and Edward (born in 1848 and nicknamed Ted).

Melville Bell later became a lecturer on elocution and speech at the University of Edinburgh. With his brother

Alexander Graham Bell's mother, Eliza, painted this portrait of his father, Alexander Melville Bell, in 1844, the year they were married.

VISIBLE SPEECH.

INVENTED IN 1864 BY

Prof. A. Melville Bell.

PRESENTED TO THE MEMBERS OF THE BOSTON SOCIETY OF ARTS, BY
A. GRAHAM BELL, 18 BEACON STREET.

Bell's father, Alexander Melville Bell, created Visible Speech, a kind of universal alphabet that reduced all the sounds a human voice can utter into a series of written symbols.

David he wrote a textbook, *The Standard Elocutionist*, which was the bible of students of public speaking for many decades. But his outstanding contribution was what he called Visible Speech, a kind of universal alphabet. Visible Speech reduced all the sounds a human voice can utter into a series of symbols. By indicating the positions of the lips, tongue, and other vocal organs, Visible Speech symbols instructed those who knew how to decipher them exactly how to pronounce any sound in any language.

One of Aleck's boyhood memories was of helping his father demonstrate the effectiveness of Visible Speech in front of large audiences. After introducing Aleck to the audience and explaining that his son knew how to read the symbols of Visible Speech, Melville asked him to leave the room. Then he called on members of the audience to produce sounds for him to transcribe in Visible Speech. After writing the appropriate symbols on a blackboard, Melville called his son back into the room. Aleck recalled pleasing the audience on one occasion by decoding the Visible Speech symbols into the sound of a woodcutter sawing wood, and on another by pronouncing a Sanskrit sound that is a cross between a K and a T, a sound that he had never before heard and one that most non-Indians had great difficulty mastering.

Proud as he must have been of his connection with his distinguished grandfather and father, Aleck nonetheless was determined from boyhood to demonstrate that he was his own man. He made this intention clear when, at the age of 11, he decided to take a middle name. He chose "Graham" in honor of a friend of his father's—a plantation owner in Cuba named Alexander Graham, who was the Bells' houseguest at the time.

Just as important to the development of young Aleck as the professional influence of his grandfather and father was his relationship with his mother. Eliza Bell's hearing was seriously impaired and she usually used an ear tube to focus sound into her ear. Aleck, alone among her three sons, had a special way of communicating with his mother. Instead of shouting into the ear tube, he would put his lips directly against her forehead and speak in a low voice. Eliza also taught him the manual alphabet, in which positions of the fingers indicate the letters. In this way, Aleck could spell words out directly into her hand.

Despite Eliza's deafness, she was an excellent pianist. By placing the mouthpiece of her ear tube on the piano's soundboard and the tube in her ear, Eliza was able to evaluate her own performance. The bond between Aleck and his mother deepened as he showed a real gift for the piano. She arranged for him to study with the best piano teacher in Edinburgh, and for a while Aleck dreamed of a career as a professional pianist. Alexander Graham Bell later said that his early love of music "had a good deal to do in preparing [me] for the scientific study of sound."

Aleck's education began at home, and he did not enter school until he was 10. By the time he was 14, he had finished his formal education. Although his grades were nothing to admire, his hobbies—collecting plants, birds' eggs, and animal skeletons and skulls—showed that he was a scientist at heart. Reflecting on these boyhood pastimes, he later wrote, "I can see in these natural-history collections a preparation for scientific work. The collection of material involved the close observation of the likenesses and differences of objects of very similar kind, and the orderly arrangement, as in a museum, stimulated the formation of generalizations of various kinds. . . . I am inclined to think that the making of these collections formed an important part of my education and was responsible for my early bent toward scientific pursuits."

Bell came up with his first invention during his schoolboy years. The father of one of his classmates owned large flour mills. One day when the two boys were making a nuisance of themselves by running around the mills, the father called them into his office. He challenged them to do something useful instead of getting in the way and suggested they try to think of a way to remove the husks from the grains of wheat. Aleck first had the idea of using a nail-brush to do the job. The boys were pleased with the result but knew it would not work on a large scale. Then Aleck recalled an unused machine they had chanced upon while wandering through the mills. Since it had a whirling brush-covered paddle inside it, why couldn't it be used to remove husks from grain? The boys tried it out and soon after proudly presented the mill owner with the cleaned wheat. In his late 70s Alexander Graham Bell still took pride in the fact that "the process . . . or a substantially similar one, has been carried on at the mills ever since."

Aleck Bell (right), with his two brothers, Melville (left), and Edward, in a watercolor done by their mother.

Despite Aleck's scientific collections and his triumph in the mill, Melville Bell was dissatisfied with his son's lackluster academic achievement. When Grandfather Bell became a widower in 1862, Melville decided to send young Aleck to spend a year in London with him. There was already a bond between the two in that they shared a birthday—March 3. On Aleck's 13th birthday, he had composed a poem in honor of his grandfather's 70th birthday. The poem began:

I am thirteen years old I find,
Your birthday and mine are the same.
I wish to inherit your mind,
As well as your much honoured name.

Now Melville decided to give the old widower a chance to bequeath his mind to his feckless namesake. As it turned out, the experiment was highly successful. Alexander Graham Bell later wrote, "That year with my grandfather converted me from an ignorant and careless boy into a rather studious youth."

The year was a lonely one for a teenager used to romping around with two brothers and assorted playmates. But the lack of camaraderie only intensified Aleck's interest in remedying his "defects of education by personal study." Grandfather Bell taught his grandson to budget his time. He had Aleck memorize soliloquies from Shakespeare's masterpieces. He allowed Aleck to sit in while he taught his students how to correct their speech defects. And he also gave Aleck the freedom of his library, where he began to read books about sound.

Grandfather Bell gave Aleck an allowance, and for the first time the young man felt independent. When Aleck returned to the family in Edinburgh, however, his father discontinued his allowance. Having had his first taste of adult independence, Aleck began to resent being treated as a boy again. Perhaps his father sensed his discontent. In any case, he issued a challenge to Aleck and his older brother to construct a "speaking machine." Before leaving London to return home from Grandfather Bell's house, Aleck had gone with his father there to see a model of a human head that, when properly manipulated, could simulate speech. Alexander Graham Bell later reflected on his father's challenge: "I don't suppose he thought we could produce anything of value in itself, but he knew we could not experiment and manufacture anything which even tried to speak, without learning something of the voice, and the throat and the mouth—all that wonderful mechanism of sound production in which he was so interested." In the end, the boys got their talking head to utter the syllables "ma-ma," with Melly blowing through the flexible tube that served as a windpipe and Aleck working the rubber lips. Their triumph was complete when they overheard a neighbor expressing concern about the crying baby.

Once the task was completed, however, Aleck again began to long for independence. Without their father's consent or knowledge, he and Melly responded to a newspaper advertisement that seemed tailor-made for them. The Weston House Academy in Elgin, on the northern coast of Scotland, had openings for two student teachers, one in music and one in elocution. Naively, the boys gave their father's name as a reference. When the headmaster contacted Melville Bell, the matter came out into the open. The upshot was that Melly became his father's assistant in Edinburgh, while Aleck—not quite 16 years old—went off to Weston House as a student teacher in both music and elocution. Some of Aleck's students there were older than he was, but he never let on. Aleck taught at Weston House Academy for two years, with a year off in the middle to take courses in Greek and Latin at the University of Edinburgh.

On his return to Elgin in the fall of 1865, Aleck began his first serious work on the science of speech production. In the meantime, Grandfather Bell had died and Melville, Eliza, and Ted had moved to London, where Melville took over his father's practice. (Melly took over the Bell practice in Edinburgh.) From Elgin, Aleck sent Melville a 40-page letter describing his work on vowel sounds, which had led him to the conclusion "that in uttering the vowel elements of speech faint musical tones could be heard accompanying the sound of the voice." Proud of his son, Melville shared the contents of the letter with Alexander Ellis, a linguist—a specialist in the science of language—who was one of the prominent scholars whom Melville had gotten to know in London. Later Melville arranged for Aleck to discuss his work with Ellis in person.

Aleck, who had believed that his discovery about vowels had never been made before, was both depressed and elated by what he learned from Ellis. In 1875 Ellis would publish an English translation of the writings of Hermann von Helmholtz, a German scientist who was doing interesting work in several fields. Ellis now told Aleck that, in an important book on sound published in 1863, Helmholtz had already reached the same conclusion about vowel sounds as Aleck had. Aleck had come to his conclusions using nothing more than a pencil, which he tapped against his cheek and throat in various positions while forming vowel sounds. Helmholtz, in contrast, had used tuning forks kept vibrating by electromagnets and a battery. Aleck was disappointed to learn that his discovery was not new— but thrilled that he had independently, and with no apparatus to speak of, reached the same conclusion as a great scientist.

Anxious now to find out exactly how Helmholtz had done his work, Aleck asked Ellis for guidance. Ellis lent him a copy of Helmholtz's work in the original German, a language Aleck did not know. The figures illustrating Helmholtz's descriptions of his experiments planted the false idea in Aleck's head that the German physicist had transmitted vowel sounds by telegraph. A few years later Aleck found a copy of Helmholtz's book in French, a language he did know. Only then did he learn of his mistake. But his misconception led him to the early conviction that not only vowel sounds, but all speech, could be sent over telegraph wires. Aleck began to experiment with tuning forks and electromagnets himself.

Just as Aleck was coming into his own as a teacher and scientist, a death in the family cast a shadow on his world. His younger brother, Ted, was the tallest of the three boys but had never had a strong constitution. Now, in May 1867, Ted died of tuberculosis at the age of 19. To be nearer to his parents in London, Aleck left Scotland for a teaching assignment in Bath, England. There he continued his work with tuning forks and electrical circuits.

The following year, Melville Bell traveled to the United States, where he gave a successful series of lectures on Visible Speech. To cover the practice in his absence, Aleck moved to London, where he also took courses in anatomy and physiology at University College. The same year, Aleck began as a practitioner of Visible Speech in his own right. Melville Bell had come to see that his universal alphabet might be useful in teaching speech to the deaf. As Alexander Graham Bell later wrote, "Persons who were born deaf might, through the use of [Melville's] symbols, be taught to use their vocal organs and speak, instead of being limited in their means of communication to gestures, finger-spelling, or writing." Aleck began as an assistant teacher in a private school for deaf children near London. His success with Visible Speech was notable, and he delighted in the news that one of his formerly speechless students now greeted her mother with the words, "I love you, Mama."

At a time when Melville Bell should have been feeling satisfaction in his own professional stature at home and abroad and in the achievements of his two surviving sons, death struck the Bell family again. In May 1870, Melly, too, succumbed to tuberculosis. Eliza and Melville began to worry about their surviving son, who seemed perpetually exhausted by all the activities he was pursuing. A visit to a specialist confirmed their fears: Unless Aleck moved to a more healthful climate, he had only six months to a year to live. Melville recalled that as a young man he had been

text continues on page 23

ELECTROMAGNETISM: THE SCIENTIFIC PRINCIPLE UNDERLYING THE TELEPHONE

When Joseph Henry was born in 1797, the basic principles on which Bell relied when designing the telephone had not yet been discovered. Henry would himself play a significant part in developing those principles. Alexander Graham Bell might not have received the encouragement he needed to see his project through if he had brought his ideas and apparatus to a scientist who was not as well acquainted with the new principles of electricity.

A telephone receiver contains an electromagnet—a wire coil that turns into a magnet when electric current passes through it. The principle of electromagnetism began to be understood less than three decades before Bell's birth in 1847, beginning with the discovery that an electric current creates a magnetic field (a region in which an object experiences a magnetic force) around a wire. This electromagnetic effect was discovered in 1820, when a Danish physics teacher was explaining to his class what was then known about electric current. Among the instruments on his desk there happened to be a compass. The teacher, Hans Christian Oersted, noticed that when he ran a current through a wire in the vicinity of the compass, the compass needle changed direction.

Oersted's discovery led to the development of the electromagnet, the simplest type of which is a coil that is made magnetic by passing an electric current through it. Electromagnets have many uses in telecommunications and other industry. For example, a crane can lift scrap metal when current flows through its strong electromagnet. The scrap can be dumped by shutting the

American physicist Joseph Henry developed the first practical electromagnet in 1829.

The scrap lifted by this crane can be dumped by shutting the current off, which demagnetizes the crane's electromagnet.

current off, because then the electromagnet is no longer magnetized.

Joseph Henry did not design the first electromagnet, but he made the first practical one, in 1829. Another electromagnet he designed, which could lift more than 2,000 pounds, set a world record for strength at the time. Henry's work with electromagnets helped scientists learn that electromagnets can be made stronger by increasing the coil's magnetic field in several ways. This could be done by putting an iron core in the coil's center or by increasing the number of turns of wire in the coil, the current in the coil, or the voltage—the pressure that pushes an electrical charge—passing across the coil.

In 1829 Henry also used his knowledge of electromagnets to construct a type of electric motor. An electric motor uses an electromagnet to convert electric energy into mechanical energy that can then perform work.

Another electromagnetic effect that Bell used in working out his early telephones was electromagnetic induction. In 1831 Joseph Henry became the first person to observe this process, through which variations in a magnetic field cause an electric current to flow. However, the British scientist Michael Faraday is given credit for the discovery of electromagnetic induction, since he published his results first.

ELECTROMAGNETISM: THE SCIENTIFIC PRINCIPLE UNDERLYING THE TELEPHONE

continued from previous page

Magnetism causes an electric current to flow only if a magnetic field is changing. (Electricity, on the other hand, causes magnetism either if a current is flowing or if the electric field is changing.) If a magnetic field that passes through a coil is steady, no current flows through the coil. But if the magnetic field changes, current does flow through the coil. A magnetic field can be changed by moving either the coil or the magnet causing the field. If the latter is an electromagnet, changing the amount of current flowing into it also changes the magnetic field.

Bell's telephone depended on electromagnetism and electromagnetic induction. The current flowing through the telephone's electromagnet is varied in strength by the mechanical vibrations of sound. The voice of the person speaking into the telephone causes air to vibrate, and these vibrations in turn cause the diaphragm of the telephone transmitter to vibrate. The diaphragm (which is either made of iron or has a piece of iron stuck to it) vibrates near the pole of an electromagnet. The vibrations cause the magnetic field to change, or "undulate" (a term Bell favored), thus causing the current in the wire of the magnet to undulate also. In other words, the changing magnetic field induces a current that is part of the circuit leading to the receiver. At the receiver the reverse effect takes place, recreating the original sounds.

text continued from page 19

restored to health by a four-year stay in the Canadian province of Newfoundland. On the strength of his previous American tour, he himself was already scheduled to travel there again for a second series of lectures that autumn. Instead of going alone and returning to London, he decided to take the remaining family with him to Canada for the sake of Aleck's health.

On August 1, 1870, the remnant of the Bell family landed in Canada. Melville had some friends from Scotland who had moved to Brantford, in the province of Ontario. The Bells bought a large house of their own there, with woods and a view of the Grand River. In his new surroundings, Aleck's health was soon restored. Soon Aleck, used to a crowded schedule of teaching and experimenting and studying, began to look for a project to fill his time. An opportunity soon presented itself. On Melville's second lecture tour in Boston, the principal of a school there for deaf children heard him describe the usefulness of Visible Speech in teaching the deaf to speak. She invited Melville to lecture to the teachers at her school. He told her that he could not, but recommended his son instead. In short order, Aleck received an official invitation from the Boston School Board. And so in April 1871, at the age of 24, Alexander Graham Bell arrived in that Massachusetts city, full of hopes, dreams, and aspirations.

"Great Discoveries and Inventions . . . Arise from the Observation of Little Things"

Aleck Bell's first American teaching position lasted, by pre-arrangement, only a few weeks. But his use of Visible Speech was so successful that before long he was in demand at other institutions where deaf children were taught. The parents of deaf children also sought him out for private lessons.

Bell's method was simple. On a blackboard he first sketched a human face. Then, using a pointer, he prompted the children to touch the same parts of their own faces as those to which he pointed. Next, using an eraser, he left on the board only the lips, tongue, and other speech organs that Visible Speech depicted. Finally, he showed them how to use each speech organ to produce different sounds. In a

Alexander Graham Bell (top right) with the students and teachers of the Boston School for the Deaf, June 21, 1871.

short time even the youngest children could sound out syllables illustrated by the Visible Speech symbols.

Helping his deaf students to speak by seeing sounds they could not hear was only one of Bell's goals as a teacher. Because he understood the physics of sound, he knew that all sounds are produced by vibrating objects. Thus he also sought to alert his students to the sounds around them by helping them feel sound vibrations. One aid he used was a simple toy balloon. By clutching one tightly against their chests, deaf children could feel the vibrations of surrounding sounds. Bell hoped that this method might even help save a deaf child's life while crossing the street after dark, when the vibrations felt through a tightly held balloon might give advance warning of an approaching vehicle.

That summer Bell returned to Canada, where he put Visible Speech to a different use. While hiking one day, he discovered a group of Mohawks in the vicinity. They were pleased with the young man's interest in their language, particularly when he offered to transcribe it into Visible Speech so that others could learn to speak it properly. The tribespeople showed their affection for Bell by teaching him their war dance. In years to come, he would celebrate personal triumphs by suddenly breaking into that dance. Mohawk chief William Johnson even adopted Bell into the tribe and made him an honorary chief.

In March and April 1872, Bell was invited to demonstrate his methods at the Clarke School for the Deaf in Northampton, Massachusetts. There he met and impressed the president of the school, a 50-year-old lawyer from Cambridge, Massachusetts, named Gardiner Greene Hubbard. Hubbard had become interested in the education of deaf children after his daughter Mabel's hearing was destroyed by a severe case of scarlet fever when she was five years old. He and his wife were horrified at the suggestion that Mabel's new disability should bar her from the life their hearing daughters led. The Hubbards had refused to accept advice that Mabel should now be taught to communicate exclusively by sign language. Instead, they had continued to speak to her and to introduce her to new words just as if she could still hear. They insisted that she continue to communicate through speech, even though her voice no longer sounded like a hearing person's. As a result of their efforts, Mabel learned to read lips skillfully. During a stay in Germany with her parents, her lip-reading skills even enabled her to learn the new language so that she was able to interpret for her parents, who could not speak German.

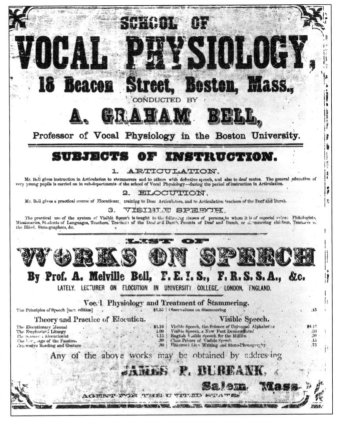

This advertisement for Bell's school of vocal physiology also includes a list of books by Bell's father.

The following fall, Bell rented rooms in Boston and opened a "school of vocal physiology." Like his grandfather before him, he advertised his skills in correcting "stammering and other defects of utterance." And like his father, he advertised his abilities in "practical instruction in Visible Speech."

One of Bell's first clients was one Thomas Sanders, a wealthy leather merchant from Salem, Massachusetts. Sanders brought his five-year-old son George, who had been born deaf and had never heard or spoken a word, to study with Bell. Soon Bell devised ingenious methods of educating the little boy. On a glove for the child's hand, he drew the letters of the alphabet and a few common words. Teacher and pupil could soon communicate with one another by pointing to different parts of the "magic glove." After teaching young George to read, Bell wrote out a storybook for his student. Unlike a hearing child, George could not hear the oral storyteller's stress upon certain words for emphasis. To compensate, Bell drew certain words in different sizes.

Bell's professional life consisted of more, however, than just visits to schools for the deaf and sessions with private pupils. He also attended a conference for educators of the deaf, published several articles on Visible Speech, and started his own magazine, *The Visible Speech Pioneer,* which he circulated to a small readership. In addition, he took advantage of his access to the scientific community of Boston to help advance his understanding of sound and electricity. On his first day in Boston, in 1871, he visited Lewis Monroe, a friend of his father's who was then a professor of elocution at the Massachusetts Institute of Technology (MIT). MIT had been in operation only since 1865, but it was already a significant scientific center. Impressed by the knowledge and curiosity of his friend's son, Monroe gave Bell a new book on the science of sound. He also told him that MIT had instruments just like those Helmholtz had used for his groundbreaking work on sound. In 1872 Bell attended a variety of scientific lectures at MIT and elsewhere in Boston, and took out books dealing with electricity from the Boston Public Library.

Bell's teaching brought in enough money to cover his basic expenses, but he required additional funds to cover the costs of equipment for his experiments in sound and electricity. In the fall of 1872 he came across an exciting news item in the same Boston newspaper in which he ran the advertisement for his school. According to the article, the

Western Union Company had paid a considerable sum to the inventor of a new telegraph system that made it possible to send two messages at the same time over the same wire. All of a sudden, the busy young man began to realize that some of his ideas about sending sound electrically might have commercial value.

Even before leaving England in 1870, Bell had been intrigued by the idea of using a commonly known musical phenomenon to transmit several telegraph messages at once. He knew that a sound's pitch—how high or low a sound seems—depends on its frequency, that is, how quickly the source of the sound is vibrating. Bell knew that every object has its own natural frequency of vibration and that high-frequency sounds have a high pitch, low-frequency sounds a low pitch. He also

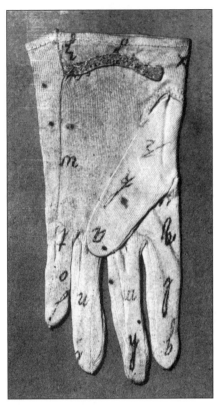

A glove Bell modified in the early 1870s as a teaching aid for his deaf pupil, George Sanders. Bell and George could communicate by pointing to different parts of the "magic glove."

knew that sound waves from one vibrating object can cause another object with the same natural frequency to vibrate. From singing into the piano in his grandfather's house in London and at his parents' in Canada, he knew that by varying the pitch of his voice he could make different piano strings vibrate in return.

He now had the idea of sending many different messages, each at a different pitch, along a single telegraph wire. At the sending end of the wire, tuning forks would be tuned to different frequencies. Each one could carry a message at its own pitch across the wire. At the receiving end, identical tuning forks would pick up only the message sent at each fork's particular frequency. In this way, what seemed to be a muddle of messages could be sorted out according to pitch at the receiving end. (Bell later began to substitute

text continues on page 33

Because of his background and upbringing, Alexander Graham Bell had a better understanding of sound, speech production, and hearing than other inventors—such as Elisha Gray of Chicago and Professor Amos E. Dolbear of Tufts University—who were also trying to convey speech electrically. Bell's deep understanding of these phenomena enabled him to develop the first "electric speaking telephone," as it was then called, even though his understanding of electricity was not as deep as that of some of his rivals.

Bell understood that sound is produced by vibrating objects and that it travels in waves. He knew that sound waves travel through air or another substance in the same way that energy moves through the coils of a spring when a section of the spring is compressed and released.

When an object moves outward as part of its vibration, it compresses the air or other substance into which it is pushing. It thus creates an area of compression. Because sound waves compress molecules (groups of atoms bonded together) of the substance through which they travel, they are called compressional waves.

When an object vibrates inward as it undulates, the air or other substance there expands into the area previously held by the object. This area of expansion is called a rarefaction.

Compressions and rarefactions move away from the source of the vibration at the speed of sound, about 340 meters (or 1,116 feet) per second, forming "sound waves." Bell knew that sound waves consist of the pattern of compressions and rarefactions created by a vibrating object. He understood that if electric currents could be made to mimic a sound's pattern of compressions and rarefactions, any sound could be transmitted electrically.

Bell knew that rapidly vibrating objects have a higher frequency than less rapidly vibrating ones—that is, they go through their cycle of vibration more times each second. A sound's frequency determines its pitch—how high or low a sound seems to a listener. Bell also understood the concept of sympathetic vibration. Such vibrations are set up when sound waves from one vibrating object cause another object of the same natural frequency to vibrate. Without understanding frequency and sympathetic vibration, Bell could not have come up with the theory behind his harmonic telegraph.

The outlines Bell sent his parents of his early lectures at Boston University indicate his thorough understanding of the mechanisms underlying human speech and hearing. A section of the throat called the larynx is covered by the vocal cords—two small folds of tissue separated by a slit. Speaking occurs when muscles in the larynx tighten the vocal cords. As a person speaks, the slit between the vocal cords becomes smaller. The vocal cords vibrate when the lungs push air over the now-tightened cords. It is these vibrations that produce the voice's sound. Speaking or singing involves continual changes in the amount of tension in the vocal cords and in the speed of the air forced from the lungs, as well as in the shape of the person's mouth. These changes affect the pitch and loudness of the speaker's or singer's voice.

In the process of hearing, sound waves pass through a canal in the outer ear and hit the eardrum, which begins to vibrate. The eardrum is a thin, soft, flexible tissue called a membrane. Its vibrations move across three tiny bones connecting the eardrum to the inner ear. Movements of the smallest of these bones cause waves in a fluid in the inner ear. The fluid then pushes against another membrane, which is covered with thousands of hair cells. The fluid's movement causes the hair-covered membrane to move and its hairs to bend. Attached to the hairs are nerve fibers that send signals to the brain when the hairs bend. These signals are then interpreted as sounds.

One of Bell's breakthroughs in developing the telephone came when he compared the movement of the eardrum membrane on the bones of the ear to the movement of a heavy telephone membrane on a piece of magnetized steel. Bell translated his understanding of the human ear into the telephone. A telephone transmitter acts just like an electrical ear, sending the speaker's words as electrical impulses. Unlike the ear, however, these electrical impulses are sent not over nerves but through wires. A telephone receiver acts like an electrical mouth. Current flowing through its electromagnet causes the receiver's membrane to vibrate. The vibrations then hit the listener's

text continued from previous page

eardrum, making it vibrate in turn. The listener's ear interprets these vibrations as the sounds spoken by the person at the other end of the line.

In honor of Bell's contributions to the science of sound, the standard unit for the intensity of sound is now called the bel. A sound's intensity depends on how much energy the sound waves carry. The decibel (dB), or one-tenth of a bel, is the unit normally used in sound and communication circuits. (Deci– is the metric prefix for one-tenth.)

For environmental noise the decibel can be expressed as a measure of the sound power level, sound intensity level, or sound pressure level. The most commonly used is the pressure level, observed on sound-level meters. Zero decibels (at a frequency of 1,000 hertz, or Hz) is said to mark the threshold of audibility, the weakest sound a person with normal hearing can discern. Since sounds of 140 decibels or higher cause pain rather than hearing, 140 dB is said to mark the threshold of pain. Each increase of 10 decibels means a tenfold increase in intensity. A sound of zero decibels is thus 100 times weaker than a sound of 20 decibels, such as a whisper. Ordinary conversation, at 60 decibels, is 40 decibels, or 10,000 (10^4) times, more intense than a 20-decibel whisper. Listening for a prolonged period to sounds above 85 decibels can cause hearing loss by damaging the inner ear.

text continued from page 29

flexible reedlike strips of metal for the tuning forks.) Bell called his idea a "harmonic telegraph." Aware that other inventors were working on various other types of "multiple telegraphs," he began to guard his equipment with great care.

In order to accomplish everything he wanted to, Bell began to work around the clock, sleeping little and eating only when famished. When he returned to his parents' home for a vacation during the summer of 1873, he was very run down and in need of rest—but he was also elated. His father's friend Lewis Monroe was now dean of Boston University's new School of Oratory and had offered Bell a professorship there beginning in the fall. Boston University had been chartered only since 1869. Now Bell, a largely self-taught man whose formal education had ended when he was only 14, would have a chance to help shape the fledgling institution. In addition to a salary, the terms of the appointment also gave him the use of a room where he could meet with his private students.

Bell returned to Boston after the vacation with renewed strength and enthusiasm. Not only would his professional status be transformed in the coming academic year; so would his relationship with both the Sanders and Hubbard families. Of the growing closeness with the Sanders family he was already aware, although he could not know where the deepening connection would lead. Despite the fact that he would be teaching more than 20 miles south in Boston, Bell had decided to give up his rooms in that city and take up living quarters that had been offered him at the Salem home of George Sanders's grandmother. In this way he could both save on rent and work more intensively with little George in whatever spare time he had. Bell continued to live at Mrs. Sanders's home for the next two and a half years. For his 27th birthday, in March 1874, Mrs. Sanders gave Bell a room to use for his experiments.

Mabel Hubbard, Bell's future wife, at age 14. They were married on July 11, 1877, when she was 20.

One of the students brought to work with Bell (and later with a teacher-in-training under his supervision) at Boston University was Mabel Hubbard. At the time of their first meeting, she was a month short of her 16th birthday. The Hubbards were at the time not living in their Cambridge house, just across the river from Boston, but were dividing their time between New York and Washington. They had arranged for Mabel to stay with cousins in Cambridge so that she could study with the young professor. Recalling their first meeting nearly a half century later, Mabel wrote in a letter to a member of the Boston University faculty:

It was in the University we first met—and that meeting stands out most vividly in my mind. I saw him first in the little green room with the window looking out on the old burying ground of Park Street Church—which then served as his office. Then we went downstairs into one of the general classrooms where he gave her first lesson to another deaf girl of my own age & I . . . watched, fascinated, his drawing on the black board of the profile of the human face which he afterwards rubbed out—leaving just those parts represented in his father's system of Visible Speech. I had never seen such a teacher as he was—so quick—so

enthusiastic—so compelling—I had whether I would or no
to follow all he said & tax my brains to respond as he
desired to his teaching of the meaning of those symbols—
Even then I flattered myself that I had been quicker than
his regular pupils to follow his explanations—& do as he
desired & that he liked me the best!

But in a diary entry describing that day written only
five years after the occasion, Mabel's analysis was a bit less
favorable. In it she recalled some of her 15-year-old's mixed
feelings about this professor of speech whose wonders she
had been hearing about for years, dating back to her time in
Germany:

> I both did and did not like him. He was so interesting that
> I was forced to like to listen to him, but he himself I dis-
> liked. He dressed carelessly in a horrible shiny broadcloth,
> expensive but not fashionable, which made his jet black
> hair look shiny. Altogether, I did not think him exactly a
> gentleman.

Within a short time, however, Mabel was writing her
mother:

> Mr. Bell said today my voice was naturally sweet. Think of
> that! If I can only learn to use it properly, perhaps I will
> yet rival you in sweetness of voice. He continues pleased
> with me. . . . I enjoy my lessons very much and am glad
> you want me to stay. Everyone says it would be a pity to
> go away just as I am really trying to improve.

During the same month that Mabel Hubbard entered
Bell's life, he delivered his first lecture at Boston University.
In it he described sound waves in air and referred to
Helmholtz's experiments to explain the properties of sound,
including pitch and loudness. He also used a large model of
the ear to clarify the workings of that organ and once again
referred to Helmholtz's description of how sound waves are
sent to the brain. Finally, he used models of the different
vocal organs, including the mouth and larynx, to show their
interaction in producing human speech.

Bell's new professorship brought him recognition from the scientific community. In April 1874 he was invited to give a lecture explaining Visible Speech to the Society of Arts and Sciences at MIT. In a letter to his parents he described how pleased he was that about 400 people had turned out to hear him speak. The lecture, he wrote, "has at once placed me in a new position in Boston. It has brought me into contact with the scientific minds of the city." Among the benefits of his new acclaim were the opportunity to collaborate with a Boston ear specialist, Dr. Clarence J. Blake, and "permission to experiment with Helmholtz's apparatus" at MIT, as well as with two other pieces of equipment there that he hoped could help his deaf students.

One of these instruments consisted of a sheet of glass covered with black pigment, along with a mouthpiece and a long wooden lever attached to a stretched membrane (a thin sheet of a pliable substance), with a bristle on the lever's edge. The bristle moved up and down on the glass whenever a sound was spoken into the mouthpiece. Its motions thus traced the shape of the sound's vibration. Bell hoped that he and other teachers of the deaf could use this instrument to show their pupils the shape of any sound's vibrations and then assist them in recreating the same sound.

Bell's first experiments with the MIT instrument disappointed him. When he complained to his friend Dr. Blake that the instrument was less sensitive than a human ear, the medical specialist gave him an actual human ear, taken from a corpse in the morgue, to experiment with. Bell used that ear to construct his own version of the MIT instrument and was pleased with its increased sensitivity.

At the end of the school year, Bell—once again exhausted from all his activities—went back to Canada to recuperate during the summer of 1874. He brought with him the various pieces of apparatus with which he had been

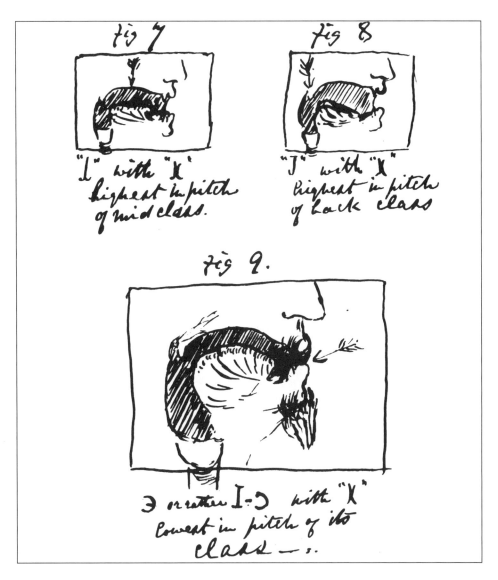

making his experiments on the harmonic telegraph, as well his human-ear-based version of the MIT instrument. While resting in his favorite spot, overlooking the Grand River, he let the various pieces of information floating around in his brain wash over one another. Forty years later he was to describe how "one observation leads to another. Starting with a very small thing . . . and following this up by other

A page from Bell's notebooks on his experiments in sound.

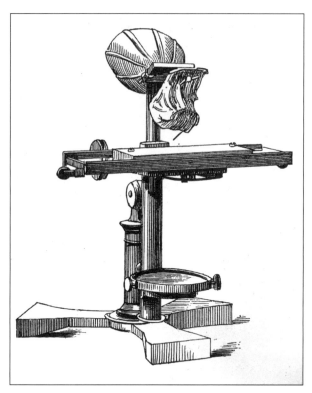

Bell hoped to use the ear phonautograph to show deaf students the shape of any sound's vibrations and to guide them in recreating the same sound.

observations—we broaden our field of knowledge and reach generalizations of considerable magnitude as the resultant of numerous small thoughts brought together in the mind and carefully considered."

Bell thought, for example, about the way a vibrating object produces sound waves in air. With each outward motion of the vibrating object the air before it is compressed, and with each inward motion the air expands into the region vacated by the object. Bell reflected on the fact that as a sound wave moves through air it thus consists of a series of compressed and expanded regions. As he recalled years later, it occurred to him gradually that, using electricity, "it would be possible to transmit sounds of any sort if we could only occasion a variation in the intensity of the current exactly like that occurring in the density of the air while a given sound is made."

Thinking about his electrical experiments, Bell also reached the conclusion that "theoretically you might, by magneto electricity, create such a current. If you could only take . . . a good chunk of magnetized steel, and vibrate it in front of the pole of an electromagnet, you would get the kind of current we wanted. . . ." He did not yet know, however, how to get such a "chunk" of steel to vibrate.

On July 26, 1874, Bell was inside his parents' house, working with the instrument designed around the human ear that Dr. Blake had given him. All of a sudden Bell realized that that instrument held the solution to the problem of how to make a current of electricity vary in density as the air does during sound production. As he recalled some years later:

> I do not think that the membrane of this ear could have been half an inch in diameter and it appeared to be as thin as tissue paper. I was much struck by the disproportion in weight between the membrane and the bones that were moved by it; and it occurred to me that if such a thin and delicate membrane could move bones that were, relatively to it, very massive indeed, why should not a larger and stouter membrane be able to move a piece of steel in the manner I desired? At once the conception of a membrane speaking telephone became complete in my mind. . . .

Bell must have described his breakthrough to his father, for part of Melville Bell's diary entry that night read "Electric Speech(?)." Based on his new insight, the young man went so far as to sketch a primitive telephone. But many months, a lot of hard work, and a number of emotional and financial crises would come and go before the initial flash of genius was transformed into a working instrument.

"Onward Irresistibly in the Direction of the Telephone"

Alexander Graham Bell desperately needed two kinds of assistance—financial and mechanical—before he could transform into a practical telephone his theory that sound could be transmitted electrically. Luckily, both forms of assistance would be provided in the months after his return to Boston for the school year 1874–75.

From his first meeting with Bell at the Clarke School in March–April 1872, Gardiner Greene Hubbard had taken a liking to the young man. Hubbard had welcomed him into his home, where the rather formal Bell—who had no sisters of his own—often found himself the butt of the four Hubbard daughters' jokes. In October 1874 Bell was invited to Sunday tea at the Hubbards'. After the meal, he sat down at the piano, as he often did. On this occasion,

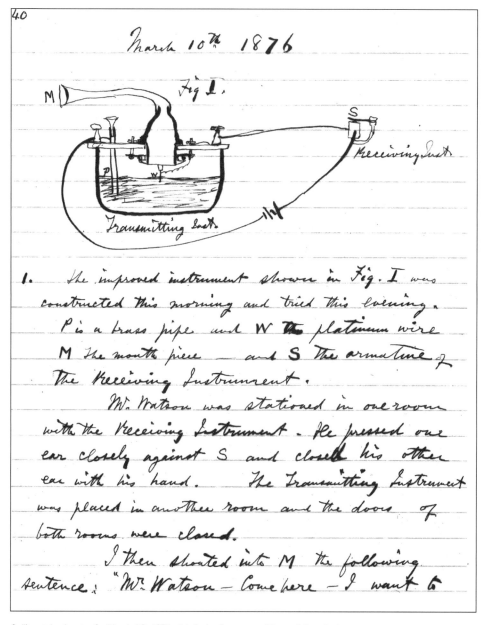

March 10th 1876

Fig. I.

M

S

Receiving Inst.

P

W

Transmitting Inst.

1. The improved instrument shown in Fig. I was constructed this morning and tried this evening. P is a brass pipe and W the platinum wire M the mouth piece — and S the armature of the Receiving Instrument.

Mr Watson was stationed in one room with the Receiving Instrument. He pressed one ear closely against S and closed his other ear with his hand. The Transmitting Instrument was placed in another room and the doors of both rooms were closed.

I then shouted into M the following sentence: "Mr Watson — Come here — I want to

Bell's notebook entry for March 10, 1876, details the first successful use of the telephone.

though, instead of merely entertaining the family, he took a moment to show that when he held down the pedal to release the strings and sang a note into the piano, the piano answered back with the same note. He also explained that if two pianos were connected by a wire, striking a note on one would cause the same note to answer back on the other. When Hubbard asked him if there was any practical value to this phenomenon, Bell said that it could make possible the transmission of several telegraph messages over the same wire. He then went on to describe his idea for the multiple telegraph.

Bell was not yet aware that Hubbard already had a deep interest in the telegraph. The telegraph, the first device to send messages by electricity, had been in use for about 30 years. To send messages over the telegraph, the letters of the alphabet were converted into a dot-dash code developed by Samuel F. B. Morse. The telegraph changed the so-called Morse code into electrical signals. In this way, messages could be sent electrically over telegraph wires.

Ever since the Civil War had ended, in 1865, the Western Union Telegraph Company had controlled the entire nation's communications system. Hubbard resented the company's high prices and was interested in setting up a competitive business. If Bell's multiple telegraph could really be made to work, it would help Hubbard achieve his goals of increasing communications traffic and charging lower rates. Hubbard offered to provide financial backing for Bell's work in return for a share in the rights to whatever patents he might take out. Thomas Sanders, the leather merchant whose deaf son George was Bell's pupil, had already made a similar offer. Sanders was agreeable to including Hubbard in the arrangement. This loose agreement among the three men was drawn up as a formal pact some four months later, on February 27, 1875. The participants did not give their informal organization a name, but historians would later dub it the Bell Patent Association.

As much as Bell needed money to help him transform his theories into practice, he also required practical assistance. Years later he described his lack of manual dexterity: "I . . . was always clumsy in the use of my hands and inefficient where tools were concerned." Bell was lucky enough to find not only mechanical ingenuity but also true friendship in a young electrician named Thomas A. Watson, who worked for the Charles Williams electrical supply firm in Boston, one of the few companies in the United States then producing electrical appara-

tus. In Watson's autobiography, published more than 50 years later, he described their fateful first meeting, when Watson was about 20 and Bell about 27:

Bell's father-in-law, Gardiner Greene Hubbard, provided financial backing for Bell's experiments with the telephone.

> One day early in 1874 . . . there came rushing out of the office door and through the shop to my workbench a tall, slender, quick-motioned young man with a pale face, black side-whiskers and drooping mustache, big nose and high, sloping forehead crowned with bushy jet-black hair. It was Alexander Graham Bell, a young professor in Boston University, whom I then saw for the first time.

As Watson described it, Bell violated the shop's etiquette by coming directly to the mechanic, Watson, with a complaint. "He was bringing me two little instruments I had made . . . without knowing what they were for or to whom they belonged. They had not been made in accordance with his directions. . . ." However, once Bell described his harmonic telegraph idea, the relationship between the two men began to flourish. By January 1875, Watson, the most skillful workman in Williams's shop, began to be assigned regularly to Bell's projects. They would work together in the attic of the shop, often late into the night. (Watson would become such a vital participant in the birth of the telephone that, in late August 1876, Hubbard and Sanders persuaded him to leave his job at the Williams shop and become a member of what came to be called the Bell Patent Association.)

At first the collaborators concentrated exclusively on the harmonic telegraph, trying to get it to perform in practice as well as theory indicated it should. According to Watson,

> In spite of Bell's hard study on his telegraph invention, my best workmanship, and, perhaps, some small notions of my own that got built into the apparatus, we couldn't make it work rightly. When we had it rigged up in the attic, if we sent a message to our hypothetical Portland station in one corner of the room, Salem in another corner would get half of it and the other half would be scattered over the other New England stations distributed about the garret.

Before long Watson learned that the harmonic telegraph was not the young inventor's only communications dream. After one particularly disappointing session with the apparatus, Bell told him about another idea he had been nursing for over a year: to convey speech electrically. Watson wrote that Bell's exact words remained engraved in his mind over the years: "Watson, if I can get a mechanism which will make a current of electricity vary in its intensity, as the air varies in density when a sound is passing through it, I can telegraph any sound, even the sound of speech."

However impressed Watson might have been with this second idea of Bell's, neither of his financial backers showed any interest in it when he introduced it to them a few days later. Instead, they urged him to focus on the harmonic telegraph and sent him off to Washington to register for a patent. Sanders paid for his train ticket, and Hubbard saved Bell hotel expenses by letting him stay at his Washington home. It was on this trip, in early March 1875, that Bell had his encouraging interview at the Smithsonian Institution with Joseph Henry. Although Bell felt duty bound to follow through with the harmonic telegraph at his backers' request, Henry's encouraging words kept him alert for any possible telephone breakthrough.

How close he was to such an advance he had no way of knowing. On May 24, 1875, Bell wrote his parents: "Every moment of my time is devoted to study of electricity and to experiments. The subject broadens. I think that the transmission of the human voice is much more nearly at hand than I had supposed. However, this is kept in the background just now, as every effort is to be made to complete the . . . telegraph arrangement." Within days, however, work on the telegraph would force the telephone into the foreground.

In 1874, Bell met Thomas Watson, a young electrician who worked at a firm that supplied Bell with electrical parts.

It was June 2, 1875, exactly three months after Bell's second meeting with Joseph Henry. This day in June was as hot as the day in March had been cold, and hot weather never agreed with Bell. As Watson put it, "It was...a day that stays in my mind as one of vivid contrasts—a black and white, gloom and sunshine, lean and fat, poverty and riches sort of day." The two men had already spent much of the day in the attic of the

Williams shop, where the heat was intensified. They were busy tuning their instruments' reeds, or thin strips of flexible magnetized steel. They had figured out that one problem with the harmonic telegraph was that the pitch of the receiver-end reeds did not always accurately match the pitch of the corresponding reeds on the transmitter end. To improve the tuning, Bell would hold the receiver reed pressed against his ear. As Watson described it,

> One of my transmitter reeds stopped vibrating. I plucked it with my fingers to start it going. The contact point was evidently screwed too hard against the reed and I began to readjust the screw while continuing to pluck the reed when I was startled by a loud shout from Bell and out he rushed in great excitement to see what I was doing. What had happened was obvious . . . that little strip of magnetized steel I was plucking was generating by its vibration over the electromagnet, that splendid conception of Bell's—a sound-shaped electric current.

From the moment the previous summer when he had conceived of the membrane telephone, Bell had worried about a possible flaw in the theory. Perhaps the human voice lacked the power to generate a current strong enough to be heard at the receiver. But now he knew that there was no need to worry. According to Watson, the barely audible twang of Watson's plucked reed would not have seemed significant to most people: "Probably nothing would have come from the circumstance if any other man than Bell had been listening at that moment but he with his mind prepared by his great conception instantly recognized the supreme importance of that faint sound . . . he knew he was hearing, for the first time in human history, the tones and overtones of a sound transmitted by electricity."

If the slight vibration of Watson's reed could produce a sound-shaped current that could activate a receiver, so could the energy of the human voice. In Watson's words, "The speaking telephone was born at that moment. Bell knew perfectly well that the mechanism that could transmit all the complex vibrations of one sound could do the same for any sound, even that of speech. . . . All the experimenting that followed that discovery, up to the time the telephone was put into practical use, was largely a matter of working out the details."

Before the two men parted that night, Watson saw a sketch of the first Bell telephone. It had a mouthpiece closed at one end by a tightly stretched membrane. Sound waves from a speaker's voice would set the membrane vibrating. Those vibrations would in turn cause an attached transmitter spring to vibrate over one pole of an electromagnet. Electromagnetic induction would then generate a current that would "vary in its intensity, as the air varies in density when a sound is passing through it." By holding an ear up to the membrane, a listener would hear what was in effect an image of the original sound.

Even though he was thrilled by this sudden development, Bell felt riddled with guilt for having spent so much of the time meant for the harmonic telegraph on the upstart telephone. Before going to bed that night, he wrote a letter to one of his backers. It began: "Dear Mr. Hubbard, I have accidentally made a discovery of the very greatest importance."

Despite the promising breakthrough of early June, the next months were among the most stressful of Bell's life. Tom Watson fell ill, and for many weeks they were unable to make progress on any front. Moreover, Bell was feeling a financial pinch. In his excitement over his electrical experiments, he had given up most of his teaching and now was short of funds. Dean Monroe of Boston University kindly advanced him his salary for the coming academic year, so there was no need to worry about starving, but the long-term financial picture looked bleak.

Most troublesome for Bell was the reason underlying his refusal to ask Hubbard for more money. He had discovered that he was desperately in love with Mabel Hubbard, who was still only a girl of 17; he was 28. In the course of the summer of 1875, Bell was an emotional wreck as he conducted his courtship. Even after learning that Mabel was giving him cause to hope, he still had to face a bitter showdown with her father. Hubbard not only demanded that Bell stop wasting time on the telephone but also ordered him to give up Visible Speech. In effect, he issued an ultimatum: Bell could give up the telephone and Visible Speech, work on perfecting the telegraph, and marry Mabel or he could persist in his ways and give her up forever. Bell wrote Hubbard a letter that barely restrained his fury: "Should Mabel come to love me as devotedly as I love her—she will not object to any work in which I may be engaged as long as it is honorable and profitable. If she does not come to love me well enough to accept me whatever my profession or business may be—I do not want her at all! I do not want a half-love, nor do I want her to marry my profession!"

The matter was not to resolve itself until Thanksgiving Day, which was also Mabel's 18th birthday. On that day he and Mabel, with her parents' blessing, became formally engaged to be married. From that time on, at Mabel's request, Aleck Bell dropped the final letter of his nickname and became simply Alec. She thought the simpler spelling seemed more American.

The country's centennial year, 1876, was a year of changes for Bell. At the end of 1875 he gave up his private classes, turned over the teaching of George Sanders to one of his teachers-in-training, and moved from Mrs. Sanders's home in Salem to rented rooms in Boston. Bell was aware

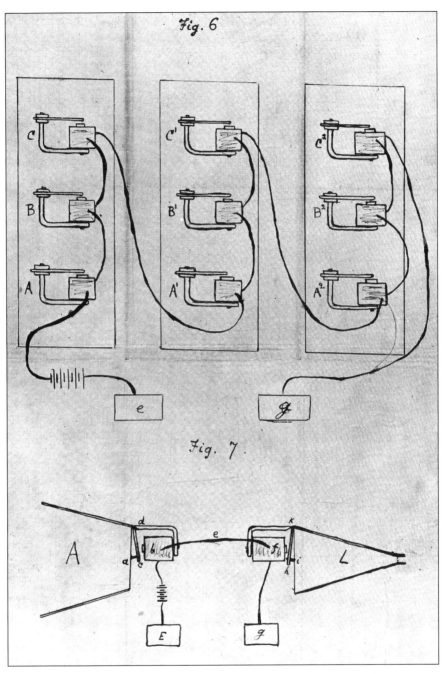

A page from Bell's patent for the telephone, issued on March 3, 1876. The top figure shows a harmonic multiple telegraph, while the bottom figure shows the magneto-electric telephone.

that other inventors were working along similar lines, and he worried that at Williams's shop his apparatus could be examined by curious eyes.

By this time, even if they were not convinced that the telephone would ever be as important as the multiple telegraph, Sanders and Hubbard were anxious for Bell to protect their investment in his invention by patenting it. But he was reluctant to do so, even though he had been drawing up the specifications for the patent since the late summer. While in Canada during the summer, in search of supplementary funds, Bell had entered into an agreement with two prominent businessmen. They had promised to file for British patents in exchange for $300, to be paid over a six-month period.

Although Hubbard was distressed that his future son-in-law had sold the British rights to his invention for such a trifling sum, he was horrified by the knowledge that a British patent would not be granted to an invention that had already been patented elsewhere. Bell felt his hands were tied: It would be unethical and counterproductive for him to work on getting an American patent as long as the Canadian businessmen were making progress toward a British patent. But as the weeks went by and the Canadians did nothing, Hubbard became increasingly nervous. On February 14, 1876, without Bell's knowledge, Hubbard went ahead and filed Bell's telephone patents.

As it turned out, Hubbard's action came not a moment too soon. That very afternoon a rival inventor, Elisha Gray, working out of Chicago, filed what was known as a caveat, or a warning to others that an inventor was working on a given project, for what he called an electric speaking telephone. Gray's caveat had the basic elements of a patent application, but he believed he could not properly apply for a patent because he had not yet succeeded in transforming his theories into practice. If Gray had filed first, Bell's

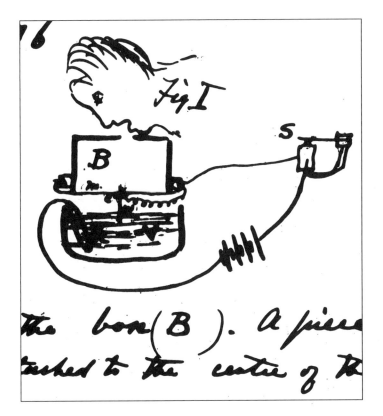

Sketches from Bell's notebook from March 8 and 9, 1876, detailing Bell's experiments with the telephone.

application for a patent might have been held up and the history of the telephone might have been very different.

Bell's patent for the telephone was granted on his 29th birthday, March 3, 1876, and officially issued March 7. It is generally agreed that this grant, U.S. Patent No. 174,465, has turned out to be among the most profitable in all business history.

At the time Bell drew up the patent specifications, and when Hubbard filed them, the telephone had yet to transmit a real message. That development would occur on March 10, 1876. The report of this event that Bell recorded in his lab notebook two days later differs somewhat from the version that Watson wrote in his autobiography many years after the event. Both men's reports agree that the telephone transmitter Bell was leaning over in the lab was a

Bell's pass to the United States International Exhibition, held in Philadelphia in June of 1876. Bell's telephone amazed and delighted the distinguished panel of scientists who judged the electrical exhibits on display.

liquid type. In a liquid transmitter a needle moving up and down in diluted sulfuric acid responds to vocal vibrations by imparting electrical impulses to a circuit containing a battery and an electromagnetic receiver. The accounts also agree that two closed doors separated Bell from Watson, who waited in Bell's bedroom with the receiver pressed to his ear. What they disagree on is the exact wording of the first sentence the telephone transmitted and the circumstances under which it was spoken.

According to Bell,

> I then shouted . . . the following sentence: "Mr. Watson—Come here—I want to see you." To my delight he came and declared that he had heard and understood what I said. I asked him to repeat the words. He answered "You said—'Mr. Watson—Come here—I want to see you.'"

According to Watson's account, however,

When all was ready I went into Bell's bedroom and stood by the bureau with my ear at the receiving telephone. Almost at once I was astonished to hear Bell's voice coming from it distinctly saying, "Mr. Watson, come here, I want you!" He had no receiving telephone at his end of the wire so I couldn't answer him, but as the tone of his voice indicated he needed help, I rushed down the hall into his room and found he had upset the acid of a battery over his clothes. He forgot the accident in his joy over the success of the new transmitter when I told him how plainly I had heard his words, and his joy was increased when he went to the other end of the wire and heard how distinctly my voice came through.

Whatever the true story, two months and many experiments and modifications later, Bell felt secure enough in the development of his invention to unveil the telephone before two scholarly groups: the American Academy of Arts and Sciences, and MIT's Society of Arts and Sciences. Although both audiences were impressed, the telephone was to have a more significant impact on an even more select group of scientists in late June.

To celebrate the 100th birthday of the United States, the country had been preparing for a Centennial Exhibition in Philadelphia. Like today's World's Fairs, the exhibition had pavilions with displays from participating countries and states. Massachusetts, like the other states, had its own exhibit, and Gardiner Hubbard served on the committee that selected the displays. Not surprisingly, the exhibit's educational section covered deaf education, including a corner set aside for Visible Speech materials.

An entire display at the Centennial Exhibition was devoted to electrical devices, but the deadline for submissions had been in April, when Bell still felt the telephone was not yet ready for public exposure. Although he now had more confidence in it, only reluctantly did he let Mabel persuade him to include the telephone in the Massachusetts educational section. Even more reluctantly did he agree to go to the exhibition, in response to a telegram from Hubbard advising that a distinguished panel of scientists would judge the electrical exhibits on Sunday, June 25. The following day Bell was scheduled to give final exams to his Boston University students, and he felt he should be available to them.

Two meetings set the stage for what would turn out to be the telephone's triumphant Philadelphia debut. The first took place in Boston on June 14 when the emperor of Brazil, Dom Pedro II, was impressed by Bell's demonstration of Visible Speech at the Boston School for the Deaf. Dom Pedro had a deep interest in education and was touring certain American schools before going to Philadelphia to join the panel of judges.

The second meeting took place in Philadelphia a week later, when Bell examined the scientific exhibits of the different participating countries. While stopping to study the telegraphic entries of his competitor Elisha Gray, he met the great English scientist Sir William Thomson, whose major contributions include the mathematical analysis of electricity and magnetism. In a letter to Mabel written that day, Bell called Sir William "a splendid, genial, good-hearted and wise-headed looking man" and described his delight "when he addressed me, to hear a good broad Scotch accent tinging his utterance!!"

The day of the judging was beastly hot. According to Bell, the judges, having made their way through the regular electrical exhibits, were ready to call it a day, thus missing his telephone equipment at the far end of the building and up a flight of stairs. Just then, Dom Pedro caught sight of him and called the judges over to Bell's display. After giving a brief explanation of how the telephone worked, Bell began to demonstrate it. Each of the judges listened in turn as Bell spoke into the transmitter at the far end of the hall.

He recited by heart different speeches from Shakespeare that his grandfather had forced him to learn years earlier. So taken was Thomson with the invention that he called it "the most wonderful thing" he had seen in America. The following December, Bell received a Centennial Exhibition award for the telephone. It came with a report signed by Sir William summarizing the judges' evaluation: The new invention was fascinating beyond the ordinary—it had "transcendent scientific interest."

The year following the Centennial Exhibition was crammed with many milestones for the telephone and its inventor. While at his parents' home in Canada later that summer, Bell made the first (one-way) "long distance" telephone call. The voices of singers and speakers at the Brantford, Ontario, telegraph office were sent over a telegraph wire to the Paris, Ontario, telegraph office eight miles away. Bell, listening at the Paris end, was thrilled when he recognized one of the performers as his father, who was supposed to have been out of town that day and thus unavailable to participate in the test.

In October 1876 Bell and Watson participated in the first two-way long-distance call, between Boston and nearby Cambridge, about three miles away. According to Watson, he and Bell celebrated their success that night by performing a Mohawk war dance. This joyful exercise did not endear them to their landlady, who "wasn't at all scientific in her tastes and we were not prompt with our rent."

As they proceeded to test the telephone over longer distances, however, not all the results were encouraging. Partly for this reason, perhaps, and partly for financial reasons, sometime in the fall of 1876 Hubbard offered the Western Union Telegraph Company all rights to the telephone for $100,000. The members of the Bell Patent Association were disappointed when Western Union said it had no use for such a "toy." But as Watson later noted, even

text continues on page 58

The word telephone comes from the Greek words for "far" (tele) and "sound" (phone). Today's telephone systems enable the sound of the human voice to travel completely around the world in a fraction of a second. Using satellites, undersea cable, or fiber-optic systems, they convert sound waves, which travel relatively slowly, into electromagnetic waves, which travel at the speed of light, 300,000 meters (186,000 miles) per second, or the equivalent of seven times around the earth each second.

The telephone acts both as a transmitter, which sends the speaker's voice electrically, and a receiver, to convert incoming electrical signals back into the sounds made by the person at the other end. The telephone transmitter lies beneath the mouthpiece; the receiver is in the earpiece.

For most of the telephone's lifetime, carbon transmitters were the type most frequently used. Carbon is not only a good conductor but is also rather flexible. It was Thomas Edison, not Bell and Watson, who designed the first carbon transmitter. (Bell and Watson tried a variety of less successful transmitters.) The carbon telephone transmitter has a thin, round, aluminum membrane and a cone-shaped chamber containing bits of carbon. On the bottom of the membrane a small, gold-plated brass dome projects into the carbon chamber.

The sound waves produced by a person speaking into the transmitter make the membrane vibrate. The vibrations are strong when the speaker's voice is loud, weak when the voice is soft. The membrane's vibrations, in turn, cause the dome to vibrate within the carbon chamber so that the dome's vibrations squeeze together the carbon grains inside the chamber. Large vibrations compress the grains more tightly than do small ones. Since an electric current passes more easily through tightly squeezed grains than loosely packed ones, more electric current flows through them when the sound is louder. Changes in the speaker's voice thus create variations in the electric current. The frequencies of the vibrations in the voice are transformed into frequencies in the electric current.

The key features of the telephone receiver are an iron membrane (often called a diaphragm), in a flexible frame, and two magnets: one a ring-shaped permanent magnet, the other an electromagnet consisting of a wire coil around a metal cylinder. The permanent magnet constantly pulls the membrane in one direction. On one side of the membrane lies the electromagnet, which becomes magnetized when electric current flows through the coil. The magnetism that results from the current's movement in one direction strengthens the pull of the per-

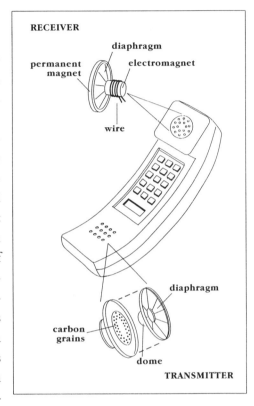

RECEIVER

diaphragm

permanent magnet

electromagnet

wire

diaphragm

carbon grains

dome

TRANSMITTER

manent magnet and attracts the membrane more strongly in that direction. The magnetism that results from the current's movement in the other direction opposes the permanent magnet's pull on the membrane, weakening the attraction so that the membrane moves in the opposite direction. This change in magnetic pull causes the membrane to create pressure changes in the air in front of it that mimic the sound waves emerging from the speaker's voice. When the sound waves hit the listener's ear, that person hears a replication of the speaker's voice.

text continued from page 55

that rejection "was another piece of good fortune for us all. Two years later those same patents could not have been bought for twenty-five million dollars."

By this time a full year had passed since Alec and Mabel had become engaged, and the once-hopeful young man was beginning to worry that he would never have enough money to support a wife. In the winter and spring of 1877, however, it became clear that many people would pay to see the telephone demonstrated, just as they might to attend an evening's theatrical performance. Somewhat to the horror of the proper Hubbards, Bell and Watson took their telephone show on the road. As Watson described the lectures,

> My function was to prove to the audiences that the telephone could really talk. . . . I also had to do something else of importance for Bell's audiences, called by courtesy, singing. Professor Bell had by his side on the stage a telephone of the big box variety we used at that time, and three or four others of the same type were suspended about the hall, all connected by means of a hired telegraph wire with the place where I was stationed, from five to twenty-five miles away. . . . My singing was always a hit. The telephone obscured its defects and gave it a mystic touch.

Preparation for a telephone demonstration in New York City also led to the development of the first phone booth. In order to see if a telegraph wire would carry Watson's voice from Boston to New York, Bell ran a trial in early April 1877. According to Watson,

> Bell was at the New York end and I in the laboratory in Boston which had a wire connecting with the telegraph office. Having vividly in my mind the strained relations still existing with our landlady, and realizing the power of my voice when I really let it go . . . I cast about for some device to deaden the noise. . . . The best I could do was to take the blankets off our beds and arrange them in a loose tunnel on the floor, with the telephone tied up in one end and a barrel hoop in the other end to facilitate my access to the mouthpiece.

Much to Watson's relief, Bell found the long-distance connection inadequate, sparing his partner the discomfort of performing for a whole evening in a blanket shroud. But Watson's pride in his impromptu invention matched his relief: "My soundproof booth was a perfect success, as far as muffling the noise was concerned, for I found by inquiry next day that no one in the house had heard the row I made. . . . Later inventors improved the booth, making it more comfortable for the public to enter but not a bit more soundproof."

Although the demonstrations never brought in much money, they did make it possible for the impoverished inventor to buy a costly trinket for his fiancée—a silver model of the telephone. It took a more substantial business deal, however, to make possible a summer wedding. A Rhode Island dry goods merchant paid Bell $5,000 for a part interest in the English patent on the telephone. With cash in hand, Alec and Mabel were married on July 11, 1877. A few weeks later, almost exactly seven years after the Bells had arrived in America, the newlyweds set off for a wedding trip to England and Scotland, where Bell would try to establish a British telephone business.

A sketch of Bell in his laboratory. Mabel painted the picture of the owl, whose nocturnal habits Bell emulated.

"A Target for the World to Shoot At"

Alexander Graham Bell scored many notable professional successes during his wedding trip to Europe, which ended up lasting well over a year. The highlight of the trip was his personal demonstration of the telephone to Queen Victoria, at the royal command.

Bell had hired an American journalist, Kate Field, to publicize the telephone in England. She did her work so thoroughly that the telephone became literally the talk of the town in London. The opening session of Parliament in 1877 featured a telephone demonstration. Articles in numerous journals sang the praises of the new invention. Even Gilbert and Sullivan, the most famous lyricist-composer team in operetta history, included a reference to the telephone in their 1878 work *H.M.S. Pinafore:*

> He'll hear no tone
> Of the maiden he loves so well!
> No Telephone
> Communicates with his cell!

In 1878, England's Queen Victoria was greatly impressed by Bell's personal demonstration of the telephone.

Bell was asked to demonstrate the telephone from the bottom of a coal mine in Newcastle and from the depths of the Thames River, wearing a diving suit. Small wonder the queen herself wanted to see firsthand this technological wonder that was arousing such interest.

And so on January 14, 1878, Bell demonstrated the capabilities of the telephone to Queen Victoria in the royal residence on the Isle of Wight. During the process, he unintentionally violated etiquette by touching the queen's hand as he offered her a telephone. The others in attendance gasped in horror, but the queen herself did not react. Her journal entry for that night merely records how impressive she found the telephone: "After dinner we went to the council room and saw the telephone. A Professor Bell explained the whole process which is the most extraordinary."

In an attempt to translate some of the public interest in the telephone into investments in a new telephone company, Bell wrote a truly remarkable document two months later. On March 15, 1878, he imagined the role his invention would play in shaping the future:

> At the present time we have a perfect network of gas-pipes and water-pipes throughout our larger cities. We have main pipes laid under the streets communicating by side pipes with the various dwellings, enabling the members to draw their supplies of gas and water from a common source.
>
> In a similar manner, it is conceivable that cables of Telephone wires could be laid underground or suspended overhead communicating by branch wires with private dwellings . . . uniting them through the main cable with a central office . . . establishing direct communication between any two places in the city. . . . I believe that in

the future wires will unite the head offices of the Telephone Company in different cities and a man in one part of the country may communicate by word of mouth with another in a distant place.

Bell derived great personal satisfaction from two other activities in which he engaged in Britain, neither related to the telephone. One brought him back to his first, enduring love—the education of the deaf. A businessman in

After providing much of the financial support for the development of the telephone, Gardiner Hubbard moved quickly to publicize its usefulness.

The Telephone.

THE proprietors of the Telephone, the invention of Alexander Graham Bell, for which patents have been issued by the United States and Great Britain, are now prepared to furnish Telephones for the transmission of articulate speech through instruments not more than twenty miles apart. Conversation can be easily carried on after slight practice and with the occasional repetition of a word or sentence. On first listening to the Telephone, though the sound is perfectly audible, the articulation seems to be indistinct; but after a few trials the ear becomes accustomed to the peculiar sound and finds little difficulty in understanding the words.

The Telephone should be set in a quiet place, where there is no noise which would interrupt ordinary conversation.

The advantages of the Telephone over the Telegraph for local business are

1st. That no skilled operator is required, but direct communication may be had by speech without the intervention of a third person.

2d. That the communication is much more rapid, the average number of words transmitted a minute by Morse Sounder being from fifteen to twenty, by Telephone from one to two hundred.

3d. That no expense is required either for its operation, maintenance, or repair. It needs no battery, and has no complicated machinery. It is unsurpassed for economy and simplicity.

The Terms for leasing two Telephones for social purposes connecting a dwelling-house with any other building will be $20 a year, for business purposes $40 a year, payable semiannually in advance, with the cost of expressage from Boston, New York, Cincinnati, Chicago, St. Louis, or San Francisco. The instruments will be kept in good working order by the lessors, free of expense, except from injuries resulting from great carelessness.

Several Telephones can be placed on the same line at an additional rental of $10 for each instrument; but the use of more than two on the same line where privacy is required is not advised. Any person within ordinary hearing distance can hear the voice calling through the Telephone. If a louder call is required one can be furnished for $5.

Telegraph lines will be constructed by the proprietors if desired. The price will vary from $100 to $150 a mile; any good mechanic can construct a line; No. 9 wire costs 8½ cents a pound, 320 pounds to the mile; 34 insulators at 25 cents each; the price of poles and setting varies in every locality; stringing wire $5 per mile; sundries $10 per mile.

Parties leasing the Telephones incur no expense beyond the annual rental and the repair of the line wire. On the following pages are extracts from the Press and other sources relating to the Telephone.

GARDINER G. HUBBARD.

CAMBRIDGE, MASS., May, 1877.

For further information and orders address

THOS. A. WATSON, 109 COURT ST., BOSTON.

Greenock, Scotland, whose daughter was born deaf, hired Bell to set up a school for deaf children, with a staff headed by a teacher trained in Visible Speech. From that school Bell wrote Mabel in early September 1878: "I have been so happy in my little school, happier than at any time since the telephone took my mind away from this work." Bell also confided in his wife that the telephone did not play a significant role in his professional hopes for the future: "I think I can be of far more use as a teacher of the deaf than I can ever be [in telephone-related work]." He remained at the school until the arrival of the teacher he had recommended. (Mabel, who had given birth to the Bells' first child a few months earlier, remained in London with the baby.)

Just before leaving England for America, Bell had another highly gratifying experience: he was invited to give a series of lectures on speech at Oxford University. Over a four-day period in late October 1878, he lectured before audiences that grew in size from day to day. Much later he was awarded an honorary doctorate from Oxford.

A catalog of Bell's personal triumphs in Britain does not tell the whole story, however. Even before his marriage and departure from the United States, things had started to go awry. In February 1877 he learned of an article in a Chicago newspaper challenging his claim to be the telephone's inventor. "The real inventor of the telephone— Mr. Elisha Gray, of Chicago—concerns himself not at all about the spurious claims of Professor Bell. . . . Mr. Gray's claims . . . are officially approved in the Patent Office at Washington, and they have already brought in large returns in money as well as in reputation to the inventor."

A few days later, Bell received a letter from Gray asking for permission to demonstrate the Bell telephone in a lecture. Gray expressed regret at having been "an hour or two behind you" in filing papers at the Patent Office but promised to give Bell full credit for the telephone.

Bell's response was an angry telegram giving Gray permission to demonstrate the telephone—but only if he stated at the lecture and published in the newspaper that the article's claims were false. Gray responded that he had not seen the article, had never spoken against Bell, and could not take the blame for everything newspapers printed. In a later letter to Bell, which Gray would live to regret, he reported that he had given Bell full credit at the lecture. He then went on to say about his role in the development of the telephone, "I do not . . . claim even the credit of inventing it, as I do not believe a mere description of an idea that has never been reduced to practice—in the strict sense of that phrase—should be dignified with the name invention."

As it started to become clear that the telephone was a very important invention indeed and one likely to prove highly profitable, all of a sudden many people began to claim a role in its invention. Rumors began to circulate that Bell had stolen the idea from others. The Western Union Company now regretted having spurned Hubbard's $100,000 offer in the autumn of 1876. Hoping to make money from the invention after all, at the end of March 1878 the Western Union Company organized a group of inventors to challenge Bell's claim to the telephone.

This group included not only Elisha Gray but also the great inventor Thomas Edison, who had been doing research on the telephone for the company for some time. Edison had recently filed an application for a patent for a telephone transmitter that even Watson agreed was an improvement over the Bell-Watson version. While working on an underwater telegraph cable, Edison had discovered that the electrical properties of carbon varied with the pressure it was under. Using this knowledge, Edison was able to design a telephone transmitter using carbon—rather than the magnets Bell had used—to vary and balance electric currents. Telephone conversations were clearer and more audible over Edison's transmitter than over Bell's. Interested customers began to rent telephones from Western Union, which the company claimed were the inventions of Edison and Gray, not Bell.

In the summer of 1878 Western Union took its campaign to tarnish Bell's reputation abroad. In articles published in France, Gray and Edison questioned Bell's integrity as an inventor. As news of the mounting attack against him reached Bell, he grew increasingly bitter. In a letter to Mabel in September 1878 he complained, "The more fame a man gets for an invention, the more does he become a target for the world to shoot at." This letter suggested his unwillingness to fight to vindicate his claim to the telephone, or even to patent any future inventions he might make: "If my ideas are worth patenting, let others do it. Let others endure the worry, the anxiety, and the expense."

But if he himself had no taste for battle, his business associates were not willing to see all their hard work and hard-earned investment amount to nothing in the face of Western Union's challenge. Just before the Bells' wedding in July 1877, Hubbard, Sanders, Bell, and Watson had formed the Bell Telephone Company to replace their earlier association. Although they knew their fledgling firm was entering into an uneven contest against a business giant, on September 12, 1878, the Bell Telephone Company sued Western Union for violation of the Bell patents. As Watson later explained, it was necessary for each inventor claiming to have invented the telephone to file with the Patent Office "a preliminary statement . . . setting forth what features of the invention he [claimed], the date when he conceived the idea and when he first constructed a working instrument."

Bell's patent for the telephone was filed a few hours before Elisha Gray (left) tried to file his. Gray battled Bell in the courts for years to try to establish his claim to the telephone.

Hubbard immediately cabled Bell in England to alert him to developments and tell him that only Bell's preliminary statement had not yet been filed. Bell's response did not encourage his partners. According to Watson, "Letters from [Bell] indicated . . . that he was disgusted with the telephone business and determined to have nothing more to do with it. In October he wrote that he was leaving England, and was going directly to his father's house in Ontario and wasn't coming to Boston at all."

The Bell Company's lawyers warned the partners that if Bell did not file his preliminary statement soon, they might forfeit their claim to the patent. To prevent this outcome, Hubbard sent Watson to meet the Bells at the dock when their ship arrived on November 10, 1878. Persuading the angry inventor to file the needed statement was not easy, but Watson—with Mabel's assistance—finally prevailed. Bell agreed to go to Boston on behalf of the company if the company paid his expenses. As it turned out, Bell had to undergo minor surgery upon his arrival in Boston, so his preliminary statement of November 20, 1878, was filed from Massachusetts General Hospital. According to Watson, "It was filed in time and, perhaps, saved his patent."

Luckily for the Bell Telephone Company, once he was over his initial reluctance to participate in the battle, Bell began to fight with vigor. Over the next two decades, Bell and Watson were required to spend much time testifying in court or preparing testimony. Watson's main role was to build reproductions of their early instruments to prove that the telephone had actually worked from the outset. Bell, too, played his role to perfection. The former professor of Boston University's School of Oratory rose to the occasion, and by all accounts Bell was one of the most effective witnesses ever to appear in a courtroom. Complimenting Bell on his performance in a later challenge to the telephone patent, one of the company's attorneys told him that "the real excellence of your deposition and its naturalness lies in the fact that in telling your own history you are telling the story of the man who invented and who knew that he had invented, the electric speaking telephone."

To find evidence to back up his claim, Bell spared no effort. He turned first to Kate Field, whom he had hired to do public relations in Britain. To help her prepare a promotional booklet called "Bell's Telephone," he had entrusted her with his scrapbook of newspaper clippings that traced the progress of his work. When it turned out that she had cut the articles out of the scrapbook and the booklet's printer could not find them, Bell was horrified, but he did not despair. He asked his parents to go through his old letters to them in search of references to his progress on the telephone. He also asked former associates if they had notes of their early work together. Some, including Dr. Clarence Blake, the ear specialist, did.

Bell also remembered that while he had been working on the description of the patent in the autumn of 1875 he had been asked to lecture on the education of the deaf at a school in Pennsylvania. He had scribbled a response to the invitation on a discarded page of his draft. When the school found the letter in its files, the date of Bell's discovery was no longer open to question.

The greatest coup of all came when Elisha Gray's letter relinquishing any claim to the invention of the telephone turned up in an unemptied trash basket in the Boston rooms where Bell and Watson had worked from January 1876 on. When Gray was asked in court on April 7, 1879, if he had in fact written the retrieved letter, he told his lawyer, "I'll swear to it, and you can swear at it!"

In November 1879, Western Union's lawyer advised the company that it could not win the case and should settle out of court. And so, on November 10, 1879, Western Union admitted the right of the Bell Telephone Company to the patent and agreed to get out of the telephone business. Watson described in his autobiography his reaction to the news: "If Bell had been in Boston I should have invited him to join in one of our old war dances. But, as he was unavailable, I had to have my dance all by myself."

Despite this victory for the Bell Telephone Company, this case was but the first of more than 600 that would be heard during the next 18 years. Some of them went as far as the Supreme Court of the United States. In every case, the Bell Company won. Nonetheless, Bell endured a great deal in the course of defending himself.

The case that disturbed him the most was the so-called Government Case (1885–92). In other cases, the only question at issue was his claim to having been the first to invent the telephone. But in the Government Case he was also charged with fraud, bribery, and perjury. Officials of the Pan-Electric Company, which had been incorporated under the laws of Tennessee to promote the telephone and telegraph inventions of one Harry Rogers, filed a suit in Tennessee charging that Bell was guilty of securing his patent illegally and unethically through collusion with Patent Office employees. The suit became known as the Government Case when the United States attorney general—who, it turned out, held a large amount of Pan-Electric stock—sued Bell in the name of the U.S. government. He claimed that Bell had known about an earlier German invention by a Philip Reis, also called the telephone, and that by claiming to have invented it himself Bell had "perpetrated the most gigantic fraud of the century."

This Reis "telephone," well known to physicists by 1870, transmitted only tones, not speech, when operated according to the inventor's specifications. As Watson later wrote, "It could . . . carry only the pitch of a sound and none of its delicate overtones. Then Bell made his revolutionary discovery of a sound-shaped electric flow." From then on, "It was an easy matter for any one to modify the Reis apparatus to accord with Bell's discovery. Then it would talk, but it was then a Bell telephone."

In the Government Case, Bell was charged with bribing an examiner in the Patent Office to show him Gray's caveat, copying from his rival's papers, and then arranging for his marked-up patent application to be replaced with a fresh copy so that his insertions of Gray's ideas would not be obvious. The case dragged on for years. To defend himself, Bell spent nine weeks in court in the spring and summer of 1892. During those weeks, he gave such a detailed statement of his work in developing the telephone that the Bell

Telephone Company, recognizing the "historical value and scientific interest" of his testimony, printed it as a book in 1908. Ultimately, the case was dropped when all the charges proved baseless.

The agony Bell endured during these years of legal battles affected his behavior for the rest of his life. He never threw anything away. Following a fire in his Washington, D.C., home in January 1887, his study was left strewn with papers. Among the men hired to clean up the mess was one named Charles Thompson, who would remain in the Bells' employ for 35 years. According to Thompson, his employer stressed that not even the smallest scrap of paper was to be thrown out if it had numbers, words, or drawings on it.

Years of lawsuits also left Bell on guard against possible misuse of his signature. According to Catherine Mackenzie, his last secretary, "He would not sign any letter that did not have its 'yours sincerely' closed up to the last written line. Otherwise, he said, something could be written in to change the meaning. . . . He never signed blank cards for autographs, but sent out a form letter with his signature attached, in response to the hundreds of requests that reached him."

Bell was also zealous about documenting all the work he later did in his laboratories in Washington, D.C., and Nova Scotia. An avid photographer from boyhood, he kept detailed records of his lab work, not only in written notes but also in photographs. He always had a lab member whose job it was to "snapshot," and he once fired a coworker for falsifying the dates on a series of photographs.

Even while caught up in the seemingly never-ending challenges to his claim to the telephone, Bell discovered that he was "a target for the world to shoot at" for other reasons as well. When President James A. Garfield was shot by an assassin in July 1881, the bullet lodged deep within the President's body. Today it would be a simple matter to locate it with X rays, but it would be another 14 years

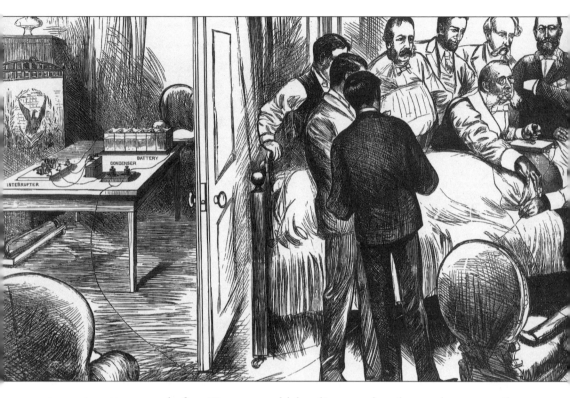

A sketch from 1881 shows Bell using his induction balance to try to locate a bullet in President Garfield's body. Bell was ridiculed after his device failed to find the bullet.

before X rays would be discovered and even longer until their use in medicine became routine. Bell, in Boston, thought he could use his knowledge of electromagnetic induction to pinpoint the bullet's location and immediately set off for Washington. There, with the help of scientific colleagues, he set about to develop an induction balance, an electromagnetic device similar to today's mine detectors. He knew in theory that passing such a balance over metal should produce a change in a telephone's tone.

After testing his new apparatus on Civil War veterans with bullets still lodged in their bodies, Bell felt it was now reliable enough to use on the President. However, two attempts failed to locate the assassin's bullet. When this news got out, Bell was mocked by rival inventors, who called him a publicity seeker and a bumbler. (Bell later learned that Garfield's mattress had steel springs, which had caused the

device to buzz over a large area. The 1881 newspaper stories mocking the inventor were thus eventually shown to be inaccurate, but not before doing their damage.)

Despite the name-calling, Bell continued to work on improving his induction balance, which was used successfully on a patient in New York in October. Meanwhile, on September 19, the President died. The postmortem showed that the bullet was so deeply implanted in his body that it is unlikely that any induction balance could have found it.

While Garfield still clung to life, the President's predicament also led Bell to design an alternative means of locating the bullet. This device, called a telephone probe, made use of a fine needle that could produce a click in a telephone receiver when it touched metal. Garfield's surgeon was unwilling to test the probe on his patient, but the device went on to be widely used until X rays made it obsolete. The University of Heidelberg eventually awarded Bell an honorary medical degree for this contribution to surgery.

Another event of the summer of 1881 proved Bell to be a target for misfortune in yet another way—not as an inventor, but as a parent. The Bells were already the proud parents of two daughters—Elsie (born in London on May 8, 1878) and Marian (nicknamed Daisy, born on February 15, 1880). Now, on August 15, 1881, while Bell was in Washington trying to help save the President's life, Mabel gave birth to a son, Edward. The newborn had difficulty

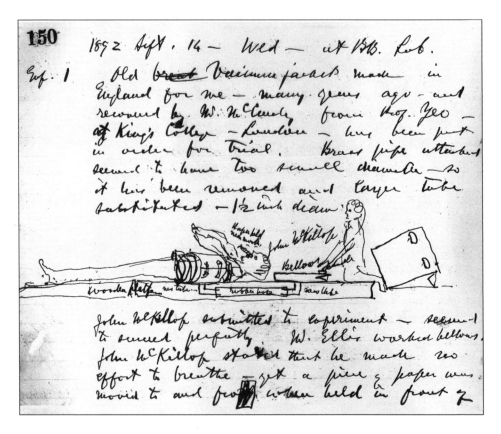

After the death of his newborn son in 1881, Bell created this metal vacuum jacket designed to force air in and out of a person's lungs.

breathing and died several hours later. The following August, after seeing President Chester Arthur, Garfield's successor, Mabel wrote her husband: "I feel as if though but for [the assassin] our own lives might have been different; you might not have gone to Washington but have stayed with me and all might have been well."

Bell responded to the death of his son by trying to do something for future victims of the same breathing problem. He designed a metal vacuum jacket, a forerunner of the iron lung, that forced air into and out of the lungs. Attached to the snug-fitting jacket was a hand bellows; by pumping the bellows, one could change the air pressure inside the jacket. Doing so would first squeeze, then release the patient's chest, resulting in regular breathing.

Alec and Mabel never recovered from their sorrow over Edward's death. Their grief was only intensified when on November 17, 1883, a second son, Robert, died just a few hours after delivery. At the time Bell was at a meeting in Hartford, Connecticut, of the National Academy of Sciences. (He had been elected to membership in the academy earlier that year.) He must have blamed himself for not being at Mabel's side in either crisis. He later wrote her, "If you were to lose a child through your own carelessness the sting would only be embittered by any reproaches addressed to you by others."

Bell's response to being a target for personal and professional misfortune was to withdraw into himself. He once wrote Mabel, "But for you I would live the life of a hermit—alone with my thought." But balancing this tendency was another inclination: to contribute to the world in any way he could. Despite the sorrows he endured during this painful period, Alexander Graham Bell continued to lead an astonishingly productive life.

5

"Science . . . The Highest of All Things"

The entry for Alexander Graham Bell in the *Dictionary of Scientific Biography* includes the following statement: "Although the telephone is not properly called a scientific invention (Bell's knowledge of electricity at the time was extremely limited), a fair proportion of the wealth he received from it was used by Bell to pursue scientific researches of his own and to support those of others."

From 1880 on Bell was involved in scientific contributions in three ways: doing his own scientific research in a variety of fields, sponsoring the work of other scientists, and organizing societies and publications to spread the results of scientific inquiry. Although he was not a religious man, he told Mabel that "Science, adding to our knowledge, bringing us nearer to God [is] the highest of all things."

From the time he moved back to the United States in 1878 and became a citizen in 1882, Bell had labs for his own scientific research in two different locations. The first and more important was in Washington, D.C., where the Alexander Graham Bells made their home not far from the Hubbards and where the Alexander Melville Bells moved to be near them. Funding

Bell was photographed in 1885 with his wife and daughters, Elsie (left) and Marian. After Marian was born in 1880, Mabel gave birth to two sons—in 1881, and again in 1883—who both died shortly after birth.

for the Washington lab came from the Volta Prize the French government awarded Bell in 1880, for his invention of the telephone. Named for Alessandro Volta (1745–1827), the Italian physicist in whose honor the electrical volt is also named, the prize brought not only acclaim but also $10,000. Although the prize had been established by Napoleon while he was emperor of France (1804–15), it had been awarded only once before. Many awards came Bell's way over the years, but he always considered the Volta Prize to be his greatest honor.

In 1881 Bell used most of the prize money to set up what he christened the Volta Laboratory in a former stable near his home. His experience with scientific teamwork had been favorable: Working with Watson on the telephone had been both stimulating and productive. And so, for the rest of his career, Bell would continue to put together scientific groups of different sizes to work on a variety of projects. This time he set up a group of three. One of them, Charles Sumner Tainter, was Watson's age and, like Watson, a former employee of the Charles Williams shop in Boston. The other was Bell's cousin Chichester Bell, whom he persuaded to give up a university position teaching chemistry in London. Bell saw himself as the group leader, whose job it was to coordinate the effort.

The most successful project of the Volta Laboratory led not to a new invention but to the improvement of a recent one. Bell's former rival Thomas Edison had already invented the phonograph, but its sound quality was not high and the records he had designed for it, shaped like cans, were hard to store, broke easily, had a short playing time, and wore out after only a few playings. Moreover, only a single copy of a recording could be made.

Charles Sumner Tainter and Chichester Bell explored different ways of recording sound and playing it back before coming up with several major improvements over Edison's invention. Instead of recording on a metal cylinder covered

with tinfoil, as Edison had, they found that a cardboard cylinder coated with wax produced better results. They also found that using a flexible needle, or stylus, recorded sound more faithfully than the rigid stylus Edison had used. And the Volta Lab associates designed round, flat records that overcame all the drawbacks of Edison's earlier ones. Just as Edison's carbon transmitter had improved on the telephone that Bell and Watson had designed, so the Volta Lab's phonograph improved on Edison's original design.

Charles Tainter dictating into his graphophone.

In 1886 the Volta associates sold the patents for their phonograph improvements. Shortly thereafter, Chichester Bell returned to England and Tainter left for California, and each went on to a career of his own. Bell used his $200,000 share of the profits to set up a research center with a focus different from that of the Volta Lab. He called this center the Volta Bureau. The bureau became renowned as a center for information about deafness.

By the time the Volta Lab associates went their separate ways, Bell knew where his next major lab would be located. In 1885 he and Mabel had gone on a vacation to Cape Breton Island, at the northern end of Nova Scotia, Canada.

There they fell in love with a town called Baddeck. Over the next several years the Bells bought up property and built an estate there. Bell called it Beinn Bhreagh (pronounced Ben Vreeah), Gaelic for "beautiful mountain." Beinn Bhreagh became a center of scientific development; many of the experiments carried out there made use of the wide-open spaces the property afforded, as well as the water around it. At these labs Bell pursued such varied interests as sheep breeding, aeronautic research, hydrofoil design, and saltwater distillation. In the late 1890s Bell also erected an astronomical observatory near the top of his "Beautiful Mountain."

Bell's passion for science carried over into his family life. As little girls, his daughters would justify knocking into each other as they walked along a street by saying they were only acting the way atoms do. And according to local lore, when his younger daughter, Daisy, had a severe case of whooping cough, Bell was able to do more to help relieve her choking than the doctor could, thanks to his understanding of the anatomy of the throat.

For all his devotion to science, however, Bell had limitations as a scientist-inventor. His interest in many things was a weakness as well as a strength, since it sometimes resulted in his leaping from one field to another without committing himself fully to any one. He liked so much to attack accepted theories that sometimes only the intervention of scientist friends kept him from publishing his own alternative views that might have drawn ridicule, such as his theory concerning the nonexistence of gravity. Not only were his mathematical skills limited, but he failed to keep up with current research in all the many fields in which he was interested. Even when he was familiar with other scientists' results, he usually insisted on reworking everything for himself. Bell continued to experiment in a variety of fields until his death, but his serious scientific publication ended by the mid-1880s.

Bell may not have been the ideal scientist himself, but he recognized scientific genius in others and often used his money to advance their work. Perhaps the most important investment he made in another scientist's research occurred in 1881, when he gave $500 of the $10,000 Volta Prize to Albert A. Michelson, a young American physicist. At the time scientists did not know that light could

In 1881, Bell gave $500 to Albert Michelson, an American physicist whose experiments revolutionized scientists' understanding of the nature of light.

travel through empty space. They believed that a substance called the ether filled all of space and that light traveled through this substance. In 1880, as a student in Germany, Michelson designed an instrument for measuring the speed of the earth's motion through the ether but could find no funding to run the experiment. Bell came to Michelson's rescue. Through this experiment and a refined version that Michelson ran six years later with Edward Morley, another American scientist, Michelson helped destroy the ether theory.

Running the experiment cost Michelson only $200. He was so honest, and so grateful to Bell, that he offered to return the leftover $300, but Bell insisted that he keep the remainder to use in further experiments. "I think the results you have obtained will prove to be of much importance," Bell told him. And in fact the outcome of the Michelson-Morley experiment inspired other scientists to set 20th-century physics on a new path. For instance, it is this experiment that is often said to have led Albert Einstein to his special theory of relativity. According to this theory, which describes the relationship among mass, the speed of light, and time, matter can be changed into energy and energy into matter ($E = mc^2$, in which E stands for energy, m for mass, and c for the speed of light).

Nine years after his grant to Michelson, Bell made another significant investment in scientific research. His close friend Samuel P. Langley had been secretary of the Smithsonian Institution since 1888. Langley, a physicist, astronomer, and aeronautics pioneer, worried that his administrative duties would leave him no time for research. The $5,000 that Bell gave toward Langley's own research was used to establish the Smithsonian Astrophysical Observatory, which flourishes to this day.

Bell not only did his own research and helped other scientists do theirs. He also understood the importance of spreading scientific results to the public and took several steps to do what he could in this regard. His time in England and Scotland had made him aware of the impor- tance of the British publication *Nature* in introducing the scientific community to new research in various fields. He believed that the scientific community in the United States could benefit from having such a journal. For that reason he and his father-in-law, Gardiner Hubbard, were willing to invest some $100,000 in the new journal *Science* over a number of years, beginning in 1882. In 1900 the American Association for the Advancement of Science named *Science* its official journal, and as such it continues to serve the American scientific community to this day.

Together with Hubbard and some 30 others, Bell was involved in the establishment in 1888 of an organization that would do much over the years to stimulate public interest in science. Their goal in setting up the National Geographic Society was "to promote the increase and diffu- sion of geographic knowledge"—that is, as Bell later described it, "to promote the study of the world upon which we live." (The founders of the National Geographic Society must have had in mind the goal of the Smithsonian

Institution, which was the "increase and diffusion of knowledge among men.") From its founding until his death in late 1897, Hubbard was the society's president. Under his leadership, it served mainly as a local science club for residents of Washington. Occasionally, it published a pamphlet for members, under the name *National Geographic Magazine,* but the articles were highly technical.

After Hubbard's death, the society elected Bell as its next president. He had a different vision for the society and its magazine. He wanted to expand membership beyond the Washington area and to publish a magazine that would be of interest to the public at large. As Bell explained years later, "We did not mean to lower the scientific standard of the magazine and make it simply popular, but we wanted to add certain features that would be of interest to everybody." To that end he hired the society's first employee, in April 1899. Describing that crucial hiring decision, Bell later said, "A young man who had made a very brilliant record at Amherst College was engaged as assistant editor of the magazine . . . to put new life into the scientific journal. . . . And so Mr. Gilbert H. Grosvenor . . . speedily captured the Society—and incidentally he captured one of my daughters." Gilbert Grosvenor, called Bert, and Elsie Bell were married in October 1900 in London, Elsie's birthplace.

In 1895 Bert Grosvenor's father, a professor of history, had published a two-volume book on Constantinople (now Istanbul) that was illustrated with 230 photographs. Inspired by this example, Bert transformed the dry, technical *National Geographic* journal into a beautifully illustrated popular magazine that nonetheless maintained the highest standards for accuracy and style. As a result, membership in the society skyrocketed, and for the first time the organization was left with an annual surplus. According to Bell in a 1912 speech at a society banquet, "In relation to our contributions to science we are now able to do what has

text continues on page 87

I n 1880 Bell produced what he considered "the greatest invention I have ever made; greater than the telephone." Although at the time Bell's opinion was not widely shared, many people now regard the photophone as a forerunner of today's fiber-optic transmission of telephone signals, as well as of today's wireless telephones.

The Photophone

When Bell arrived in England on his wedding trip, he found that a number of scientists there were excited about a recently discovered property of the element selenium. Depending on how strong a light was focused on it, the element's electrical resistance, or opposition to the flow of an electric current, varied. In May 1878, Bell told the Royal Institution, a scientific organization founded in 1799 "for the Dissemination of Useful Knowledge," that "if you insert selenium in the telephone battery and throw light upon it you change its resistance and vary the strength of the current you have sent to the telephone, so that you can hear a shadow."

When Bell returned to the United States, he became involved in the first telephone lawsuit. Although legal matters took up much of his time, he hired an associate, Charles Sumner Tainter, to help him transform his new idea into practice. Tainter moved from the Boston area to Washington, D.C., to work on the problem with Bell. Together they succeeded in devising the apparatus Bell called the photophone, from the Greek words for "light" and "sound." They placed a sensitive crystal of selenium in a telephone circuit. Near it they set up a thin mirror that vibrated in response to the sound of the voice. A beam of light was directed onto the front of the mirror. Speaking into the back of the mirror made the beam of light vibrate. Bell and Tainter used lenses to direct the beam of light from the mirror onto the selenium crystal. The variations in the light changed the resistance of the selenium and thus made the sound-shaped electric current that Bell's telephone had also required.

On April 1, 1880, Tainter sent a photophone message 213 meters (233 yards) from the top of a school building to a window of Bell's Washington

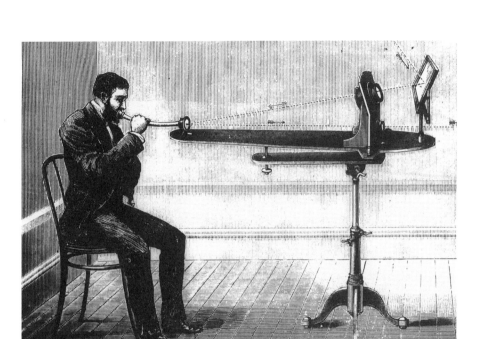

Bell's photophone was able to transmit sound over a beam of light. It may be considered a forerunner to today's wireless telephones.

lab. In response to his message—"Mr. Bell, if you hear what I say, come to the window and wave your hat"—Tainter soon saw Bell carrying out his instructions to a T.

Fiber Optics

The usefulness of the photophone was limited, but nearly a century later scientists and engineers did invent a way to transmit telephone messages over a light beam. After the development of the laser in the late 1950s, the Bell System began to work on ways to use the special properties of laser light to carry telephone calls, computer data, and video signals. The development of fiber-optic technology made it possible by the late 1970s to transmit messages by beaming laser light through narrow glass threads called optical

text continued from previous page

fibers. Such fibers, which are thinner than a single hair strand, are now being used more and more to replace copper telephone wires.

Optical fibers improve on the previous wiring system in several ways: they take up much less space beneath city streets; a fiber can carry many more messages than a copper wire, since messages are carried through fibers by short pulses of light instead of varying electrical signals through copper; static has no effect on laser beams moving through fibers, whereas it can distort messages traveling through copper wires; and signals traveling through optical fibers need to be strengthened much less frequently than those passing through copper wire.

In 1916, when asked to say something about his favorite invention, Bell told a group of trustees and faculty members of Boston University that the photophone "is the application of the principle of a beam of light as a substitute for a wire." Fiber-optic technology has made the principle behind the photophone an important part of today's telephone service, even though Bell's invention itself had little impact. Completing his thought for the same group of people, Bell said that "the photophone is nothing more nor less than wireless telephony." Today's wireless phones make use of radio, telephone, and computer technology that was unavailable to Bell when he invented the photophone.

Bell was amazed by the progress made in telephone technology even during his lifetime. When making or receiving a call, he would sometimes muse upon how far the instrument had come since he had begun to work out his early plans. Today's optical-fiber telephone transmission and wireless telephones make it clear that ever since Bell invented the first telephone it has been an invention that continues to be perfected.

text continued from page 83

not been possible for us before—contribute substantially to the support of geographic research, under the direction of our Research Committee." To this day the National Geographic Society, through its Committee for Research and Exploration, funds scientific projects in fields ranging from astronomy to vulcanology, anthropology to oceanography.

Bell gave up the presidency of the society in 1903, but that year he helped Bert Grosvenor make a crucial decision. The photographs accompanying an article Grosvenor was considering for publication included one of a woman wearing nothing above the waist. He asked his father-in-law's advice on whether it would be appropriate to publish such a photo. Bell helped him conclude that in a magazine devoted to reliable information it was more important to represent the facts truthfully than to yield to a prudish propriety. Bell, who continued as a trustee of the society until his death in 1922, remained proud that "there has never been in the history of the world a scientific society that has increased in influence and power as the National Geographic Society."

In addition to spreading scientific knowledge to large numbers of people through organizations and journals, Bell also wanted more intimate exchanges of research results. In 1891, when he and Mabel built a home in Washington, he included a room where he could play host to weekly gatherings of a dozen or so scientists. According to a friend, the noted explorer and journalist George Kennan, these informal receptions were delightful:

> There was always a definite program, planned and arranged by Mr. Bell himself, but the programs were infinitely varied and covered almost every known field of exploration and research. If a man had done, planned, or found out something new, it was always at one of Mr. Bell's "Wednesday evenings" that he first made it known. Usually, one of the scientific men would talk or read a

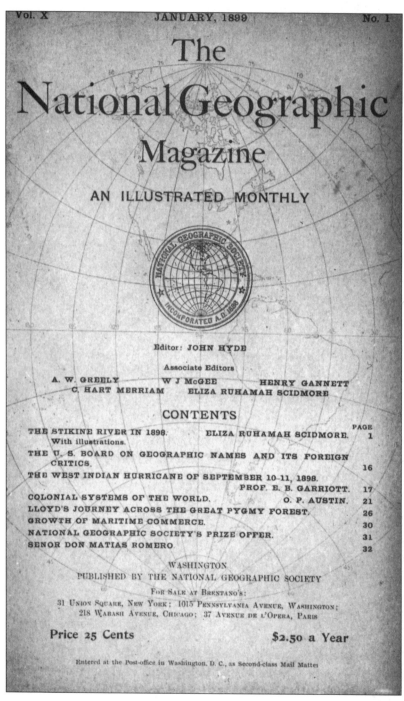

The cover of the January 1899 issue of National Geographic. *After Bell became president of the National Geographic Society in 1897, he hired Gilbert H. Grosvenor to work on* National Geographic.

paper on some subject that he had recently studied or investigated. Then the experts present would discuss it, ask questions, or make pertinent comments and suggestions. The subjects presented were of great diversity and ranged from the indigenous races of China to the life history of eels, and from the latest volcanic eruption to cancerous growths in living plants with highly interesting specimens.

Bell's younger daughter, Daisy, met her future husband through a combination of the National Geographic Society and the "Wednesday evenings." Bert Grosvenor had heard positive reports concerning the international research of botanist David Fairchild and invited him to give a lecture to the society in 1903. Expecting him to be an elderly scientist, Bert was surprised when the well-traveled botanist turned out to be only 34. Much impressed with Fairchild's lecture, Bell invited the young man to a "Wednesday evening." There the botanist met Elsie and Mabel. The following year, Elsie invited Fairchild to dinner and seated him next to her sister Daisy, who was just back from studying art in New York. In April 1905 Daisy and David were married. In their professionally distinguished and personally devoted sons-in-law, Mabel and Alexander Graham Bell found the sons they had wanted so deeply.

Even through the last years of his life Bell involved himself in a flurry of scientific activity. In a letter to Mabel written while he was testifying in one of the telephone patent cases, he hinted at the reason he felt compelled to continue his involvement in science: he begged her to "make me describe and publish my ideas that I may at least obtain credit for them and that people may know that I am still alive and working and thinking. I can't bear to hear that even my friends should think that I stumbled upon an invention and that there is no more good in me." In order to prove his worth to others, for nearly half a century after his invention of the telephone Bell continued to make important advances in a wide variety of fields.

In 1884, Bell opened a school for deaf children in Washington, D.C. Everything in the deaf students' classroom was labeled with its name in both Visible Speech and the regular alphabet.

CHAPTER 6

"My Life Work . . . The Teaching of Speech to the Deaf"

Alexander Graham Bell pursued many interests over a long lifetime, but one concern motivated him from youth on. When asked his profession, he would always answer "teacher of the deaf." Many people believe that his most significant contribution to basic science was not his invention of the telephone but rather his work on deafness. Bell not only did significant research on deafness and promoted the best interests of the deaf but also, over the course of his lifetime, devoted almost half a million dollars to benefit the deaf.

In Bell's opinion, the most striking aspect of the problem of deafness was how it isolated its victims from the rest of society. He therefore made it his personal crusade to break down the barriers that kept deaf people from mingling with the hearing world. In 1887 he made a speech that vividly describes his empathy for the deaf:

Who can picture the isolation of their lives? When we go out into the country and walk in the fields far from the city we think we are solitary; but what is that to the solitude of an intellectual being in the midst of a crowd of happy beings with whom he can not communicate and who can not communicate with him. I know that the most lonely place on the face of the earth is the heart of the city of London. I have stood on the sidewalk and seen hundreds and thousands of people pass by me, and not known a soul, and the sense of loneliness in the midst of so many is oppressive. How then must have been the loneliness of the deaf child in [past] ages?

Bell strongly believed that deaf people should not be kept to themselves but should play, study, and work with those whose hearing was not impaired. Toward this end he favored educating deaf children in day schools rather than residential institutions. He felt that boarding schools separated deaf children from hearing members of their families and from other hearing children. In the ideal day school, deaf students could not only receive special training to help them overcome their disabilities but could also mix with other children and learn to understand them by reading their lips. After all, his deaf wife, Mabel, had been educated alongside her sisters and other children with normal hearing, and she had learned to read lips so well that she functioned unobtrusively both within the family and with others.

Following his happy experience in 1878 with the school for deaf children in Greenock, Scotland, Bell decided to start a similar day school for deaf children in Washington, D.C. However, telephone-related business kept him from acting on his decision until early 1883. In October of that year Mr. Bell's Primary School opened with six deaf students in a single classroom in a house in Washington. On the first floor of the same house a local kindergarten met, and the two groups of students played together at recess time. Bell's daughters, Elsie and Daisy, were both enrolled in the kindergarten. The deaf children's classroom was designed to appeal to the senses of both sight and touch. Everything was labeled with its name in both Visible Speech and the regular alphabet. By watching the teacher pronounce the names, little by little the children began to lip-read. Bell also arranged a class for the deaf students' parents so that they could continue to work at home with the children, following the same philosophy on which the classroom work was based.

Unfortunately, the school lasted only a little more than two years. Although Bell had hoped to have a long-term teacher who would gain experience over time, his first teacher left after a year to get married, and her successor left the next year. However, the main reason for giving up the school was the attack on his character in the so-called Government Case. Bell felt he had to concentrate on clearing his name. When he closed the school, he told Mabel that he felt as if his entire life had been "shipwrecked."

Despite his personal disappointment, though, Bell continued to work to establish day schools for the deaf. In part as a result of his efforts to convince state governments to support such schools, the day school movement prospered. When the city of Chicago opened the Alexander Graham Bell School in 1918, Bell could truly feel that his ship had come in, however belatedly. This public school had separate classrooms for deaf and hearing children, but the two groups joined together at playtime, as in Bell's own Washington school.

Although Bell lacked the technical expertise needed to devise a hearing aid to help deaf people function more normally in the hearing world, he was able to design an instrument to measure the sharpness and range of people's hearing. In devising this instrument, called an audiometer, Bell again made use of the principle of electromagnetic

Edward Gallaudet clashed frequently and publicly with Bell over issues involving the deaf. Gallaudet supported teaching the deaf to communicate primarily through sign language, a practice Bell firmly opposed.

induction, which had been crucial to his invention of the telephone. In this case, a current was induced in a wire coil in circuit with a telephone receiver. By varying the intensity of the transmitted sound, a tester could compare the hearing abilities of different individuals.

Thanks to Bell's audiometer, it was now possible to detect minor hearing problems in many public school students. The audiometer also revealed that some students who had been previously thought to be completely deaf in fact had some ability to hear.

Bell believed passionately in the importance of teaching the deaf both to read lips and to speak, or "articulate," in order to help them live as comfortably as possible among the hearing. When babies are born with normal hearing, they learn to speak by copying what they hear. This is why deaf babies do not learn to speak naturally. Bell insisted that both deaf children and deaf adults could be taught to speak if they were shown how to use their speech organs, which were not affected by their deafness. After meeting Mabel and seeing how successful the training in lipreading and articulation could be, he became permanently committed to both causes.

This intense professional commitment brought Bell into bitter conflict with another leader in the education of the deaf, Edward Gallaudet, who was 10 years older than Bell. Gallaudet was not opposed to teaching lipreading and articulation, but he firmly believed that not all deaf people could master those skills well enough to have them serve as their main means of communication. For this reason, he advocated teaching the deaf to communicate through sign language.

Bell strongly opposed sign language. Because it was much easier for the deaf to learn, he believed that sign language would undermine their determination to master speech. Bell also insisted that sign language would isolate the deaf both socially and intellectually. Since most hearing people do not learn sign language, he was convinced that deaf people skilled in signing but not in lipreading and articulation would be able to communicate only with one another. Because sign language is not as precise and subtle as spoken language, Bell felt that people trained to think and speak only with sign language could never achieve the range of thought and expression open to those trained in a spoken language.

Bell himself had learned sign language early in his career as a teacher of the deaf. If he met a deaf person who would otherwise have been excluded from a conversation, he would include that person by interpreting in sign. Nevertheless, he felt that to train children to rely on signing was to do them a great disservice. It might be easier for them to master, but he felt that their options at the end of their education would be much narrower than if they had persisted in studying lipreading and articulation.

Despite their sharp disagreement over this issue, Gallaudet and Bell had much in common. They both had deaf mothers and famous fathers. In fact, Gallaudet's father had founded, in Hartford, Connecticut, the first permanent school for the deaf in America. Both men also headed professional organizations committed to the education of the deaf. Gallaudet was a leader of the American Convention of Instructors of the Deaf, to which Bell belonged. In 1890 Bell founded another professional group, the awkwardly titled American Association for the Promotion of the Teaching of Speech to the Deaf (AAPTSD).

Before their professional disagreements eventually turned bitter, these two giants in educating the deaf showed their respect for each other in several ways. While Bell was still teaching and inventing in Boston, they discussed the possibility of his joining the faculty of the college for deaf students Gallaudet headed in Washington, D.C. (This school, which was renamed for Gallaudet's father in 1894, was then the world's only one offering a college education to deaf students.) In 1880 Gallaudet's college granted Bell his first honorary degree.

In January 1891 the cordial relations between Bell and Gallaudet began to deteriorate. Gallaudet was then seeking government funding to set up at his college a school to train people with normal hearing to teach the deaf. Bell was distressed at the thought that the school might eventually admit deaf students, even though Gallaudet said he had no intention of doing so. Bell understood that deaf teachers might well have much to contribute to deaf students. Still, he knew that deaf teachers would never be able to teach deaf students what he saw as the key to their entry into a hearing society: articulation.

Gallaudet's diary entries in the first months of 1891 reveal his growing distrust of and distaste for Bell. In the entry for February 21, for instance, he wrote: "Every day lowers Bell in my esteem." Despite Bell's disapproval, Gallaudet was able to start the teacher–training program. True to Gallaudet's promise, only hearing students were admitted and taught how to teach the deaf to lip-read and articulate. Bell's fears did, however, prove well grounded over the long run: Today, Gallaudet College's teacher-training program does enroll many deaf students.

In 1895 Gallaudet was elected president of the American Convention of Instructors of the Deaf. At the

The American Convention of Instructors of the Deaf at its annual meeting in 1874. These conventions were often the scene of heated debates over the best ways to educate the deaf.

convention's meeting that summer he delivered a personal attack on Bell. To find himself even in his most beloved profession "a target for the world to shoot at" must have been a bitter blow to Bell. Nonetheless, when Bell spoke to the convention he did not return the charges. He simply said that Gallaudet had misunderstood his intentions with regard to educating the deaf. One of Bell's supporters wrote in a letter to Mabel that "he [Bell] spoke as if inspired. . . . Not a word of retaliation." Gallaudet ungenerously attributed the shortness of Bell's response to the weakness of the case on his behalf, and then went on both to revoke Bell's membership in the organization and to mock the AAPTSD by laboriously writing its lengthy name out over a wide blackboard in front of an audience of deaf people.

A few years later Bell extended a hand that enabled the two men to put their differences behind them: He asked Gallaudet to support him in his work of framing appropriate questions for the takers of the 1900 census to obtain the most useful information possible about the deaf population of the United States. The next day Gallaudet was a guest in the Bell home.

Although the two men never clashed publicly again, the professional difference that caused the rift between them still cuts through the movement for educating the deaf in America. Some educators continue to believe, with Bell, that articulation and lipreading should be the goal and sign language should not be taught. Others, following Gallaudet, believe that an approach combining oral skills with sign language is more appropriate for large numbers of deaf people. Today a growing number of activists within the deaf community believe in teaching sign to deaf children as their first language, with written English as their second, and little emphasis on spoken English.

Bell had reason to believe that deaf people could function well in the hearing world. Both his mother and his wife were deaf women who married hearing men and gave birth to children with normal hearing. He presumed that if deaf people interacted only with one another, they would be likely to marry other deaf people, which led him to worry that the offspring of such marriages would tend to be deaf.

In 1878, shortly after Bell's return from England, the Massachusetts State Board of Health asked for his assistance in gathering statistics on birth defects. As a result, he began to study genealogical records. By 1883 Bell had enough data to conclude in a paper given to the National Academy of Sciences that more deaf children were born to deaf parents than to the general population. He called for further work to be done in this area. Then he turned his data over to another researcher, who 12 years later issued a work concluding that marriages among the deaf indeed yielded many more deaf children than marriages among hearing people. If either parent had deaf relatives, the proportion of deaf children increased. And even if there were no other deaf relatives, the parents ran a higher risk of producing deaf children if they were related to one another. Many specialists in the field have since come to believe that Bell's 1883 paper and the 1895 study based on his data were 19th-century America's most important studies of human heredity.

Bell's research was controversial in the deaf community at the time, and the underlying assumptions remain controversial to this day. At the time many deaf people took offense at the title of Bell's 1883 paper, "Memoir upon the Formation of a Deaf Variety of the Human Race." They felt it implied that the deaf were somehow an inferior group of people and that the world would be a better place without them. In fact, not everyone then shared Bell's view that deafness was abnormal and that integration into the hearing world was the appropriate goal for all deaf people.

Today this rejection of Bell's operating principle is, if anything, even more pronounced. Many deaf people now are intensely proud of their culture and feel that the world is a richer place for having deaf people in it. Some even resist technological advances that could help improve defective hearing. "Let the deaf be deaf!" is their marching cry. Unlike Bell, Gallaudet did not consider deafness abnormal, which helps explain why many of the deaf preferred to ally themselves with Gallaudet against Bell.

In order to help handle all the data involved in his genealogical research, Bell hired a librarian-research assistant. Work on the project had begun in a room in Bell's Volta Laboratory, so he designated that room the Volta Bureau. Soon he recognized that the bureau was becoming a center "for the increase and diffusion of knowledge relating to the deaf." His parents, believing that the importance of the bureau's work merited a building of its own, made a $15,000 contribution, and in 1893 the Volta Bureau moved into its own handsome building. Then, in 1908, the bureau merged with the AAPTSD, and finally, in 1956, the joint

Bell's natural scientific curiosity led him from a study of heredity among the deaf to a vast program of sheep-breeding experiments on his Nova Scotia estate.

operation took on a new name: the Alexander Graham Bell Association for the Deaf. The association still flourishes in Washington, D.C., as an international center for information about deafness.

Bell's studies of heredity among the deaf led him into two other scientific inquiries, one more unusual than the other. On the vast expanses of Beinn Bhreagh, his estate in Cape Breton, Nova Scotia, Bell began sheep-breeding experiments in 1890 that continued for nearly 20 years beyond his death. In his "Sheepville," Bell crossbred sheep with more than one set of nipples, in hopes of increasing the number of twins and triplets born. Such an increase, he reasoned, would benefit not only the sheep farmers of Nova Scotia but also the larger number of people around the world who ate the meat of the sheep and relied on their wool for clothing and blankets.

In Bell's later years he also began to study the question of human longevity—specifically, whether people could inherit from their parents the tendency to live a long life. In a pamphlet he published in 1918 Bell concluded that although one could not inherit longevity, one could inherit an ability to resist disease that was probably related to longevity.

Bell's interest in the deaf as a group did not keep him from close involvement with a number of deaf individuals. In addition to his wife, Mabel, Bell also maintained contact over the years with another former student, George Sanders, whose father had joined Mabel's father in supporting Bell's early telegraph and telephone experiments. Bell was disappointed, but understanding, when George married a deaf woman, and he generously set George up in the printing business.

Among the most fruitful of Bell's personal associations with deaf individuals was one that began in 1887. Early that year, Captain Arthur H. Keller, a newspaper editor from Alabama and a former Confederate officer, brought his six-year-old daughter Helen to meet Bell in Washington, D.C. When Helen was only a year and a half old, a serious illness had destroyed her sight and hearing. Her parents had no idea how to raise and educate her. Over the years she had become, as she later described herself, "Wild and unruly, giggling and chuckling to express pleasure; kicking, scratching, uttering . . . choked screams . . . to indicate the opposite." Bell suggested that her father contact the Perkins School for the Blind in Boston. That school's director recommended that the Kellers hire a recent graduate of the school, Anne Sullivan. The subsequent interaction of teacher and student transformed Helen from a self-centered, wild child into a thinking and caring individual who could write, read Braille, and speak. After graduating in 1904 with honors from Radcliffe College, one of the finest institutions for women's education in the world, Helen Keller proceeded to work for others through associations such as the American Foundation for the Blind.

Keller also went on to write a number of books, including *The Story of My Life,* in which she wrote of her first meeting with Bell, "I did not dream that that interview would be the door through which I should pass from darkness into light." The relationship between Keller and Bell meant a great deal to both of them over the years. In 1893, 12-year-old Helen turned the first shovelful of earth at the dedication of the site for the Volta Bureau's new building. In 1896 she told the AAPTSD summer convention: "If you knew all the joy I feel in being able to speak to you today, I think you would have some idea of the value of speech to the deaf." She dedicated her autobiography in 1902 "To ALEXANDER GRAHAM BELL. Who has taught the deaf to speak and enabled the listening ear to hear speech from the Atlantic to the Rockies."

In 1907 Bell helped Keller in a time of professional need. She was scheduled to give a speech in New York at a meeting for the blind. Anne Sullivan, who normally repeated her speeches to make sure everyone could understand them, was ill and would be unable to do so. Keller sent a telegram to Bell pleading that "teacher has bad cold and cannot speak. Will you stand beside me and repeat my speech so that all may hear?" In response, Bell canceled other plans to be at her side. Years after Bell's death, Keller described just what it was about Bell that inspired her love for him: "I knew he considered me a capable human being, and not some sort of pitiable human ghost groping its way through the world."

Bell with Helen Keller (left) and her teacher, Anne Sullivan. Bell's relationship with Keller began in 1887, when Keller was six years old.

On one occasion Bell confided in Keller, "One would think I had never done anything worthwhile but the telephone. That is because it is a money-making invention. It is a pity so many people make money the criterion of success." In 1916, six years before his death, the inventor of the telephone made clear again that, proud as he was of that invention, he was prouder still of other contributions he had made: "Recognition of my work for and interest in the education of the deaf has always been more pleasing to me than even recognition of my work with the telephone."

The wide-open spaces of his Nova Scotia estate gave Bell plenty of room to fly his massive kites. Bell's experiments with kites were the first step in his quest to design a flying machine.

"The Age of the Flying Machine Was at Hand"

When people think about early experiments in aviation, the individuals whose names most readily come to mind are Orville and Wilbur Wright. On December 17, 1903, at Kitty Hawk, North Carolina, these two brothers from Dayton, Ohio, made the world's first flight in a heavier-than-air machine, which they had invented and designed themselves. Few people are aware, however, that Alexander Graham Bell was also a pioneer of aviation. The Arctic explorer Robert E. Peary wrote in 1918 that Bell, "whose name is more frequently associated with other great gifts to humanity, . . . in an unspectacular way was a potent factor in advancing man's mastery of the air."

Bell's interest in "getting into the air" went all the way back to his early years in Scotland. "For many years—in fact, from my boyhood—the subject of aerial flight has had a great fascination for me," Bell told the Washington Academy of Sciences nearly three years after the Wrights' historic flight. And in his autobiography Tom Watson recalled Bell's fascination with manned flight, even while the two men were working day and night on the harmonic telegraph and its offshoot, the telephone:

> From my earliest association with Bell he discussed with me the possibility of making a machine that would fly like a bird. He took every opportunity that presented itself to study birds, living or dead. . . . One Sunday we found a dead gull on the beach. . . . Bell spread it out on the sand, measured its wings, estimated its weight, admired its lines and muscle mechanism, and became so absorbed in his examination that, fastidious as he always was, he did not seem to notice that the specimen had been dead some time. As I was less enthusiastic I was obliged to keep well to windward of the bird during the discussion.

Watson also speculated that, had Bell had the money, "he might have dropped his telegraph experiments and gone into flying machines at that time." Before leaving for his wedding trip in Great Britain, "Bell was so certain that flying was practicable" that he made Watson agree to go into the flying machine business with him as soon as the telephone company had established itself. All the lawsuits that faced the fledgling Bell Telephone Company on Bell's return from England prevented the two men from ever collaborating on aviation experiments, however.

Even while honeymooning, Bell found time to think about flying machines. On September 27, 1877, Mabel wrote to her mother:

> What a man my husband is! I am perfectly bewildered at the number and size of the ideas with which his head is crammed. Flying machines to which telephones and torpedoes are to be attached occupy the first place just now from the observation of seagulls and the practicability of attaching telephones to wire fences. His mind is full of both of these things. Every now and then he comes back with another flying machine which has quite changed its shape within a quarter of an hour.

Bell did not begin to transform his fanciful thoughts about flying machines into experiments until 1891. By that time, much of the telephone testimony lay behind him. More importantly, in that year Bell heard Samuel Langley lecture on aviation at the National Academy of Science. Langley, an astronomer and physicist who had been secretary of the Smithsonian Institution since 1888, greatly impressed Bell and the two became close friends. Bell provided Langley with the financial and personal support he needed to continue his experiments with heavier-than-air machines. In a letter to Mabel on June 15, 1891, Bell described his excitement after Langley put on a demonstration for him: "Langley's flying machines . . . flew for me today. I shall have to make experiments upon my own account in Cape Breton. Can't keep out of it. It will be all UP with us someday!"

Samuel Langley, one of the pioneers of aviation, received financial support from Bell to continue his work on a flying machine.

Mabel was at least as enthusiastic about aviation as her husband was. In June 1893 she wrote Bell poignantly: "I am very much interested in your flying machines. At last you have come up with something I can understand." So happy was she with his work during this period that she put up no fuss when he removed some slats from a pair of new Venetian blinds she had special-ordered from Halifax for use in an experimental propeller.

As Bell experimented with a variety of rockets and rotors (systems for rotating winglike surfaces), his enthusiasm only grew, even though he was making no real progress. At one point he dictated to his secretary his ideas for "The Flying Machine of the Future; as conceived in 1892" in which he envisioned the type of helicopter that would come into use a half century later. He made a variety of attempts at rocket propulsion and worked hard to produce an appropriate fuel. A drawing in his notes gives a comic clue to the dangerous nature of some of his experiments, with one figure hiding behind a tree looking at a whirling blade while a second figure (Bell himself?) takes notes.

He also experimented with jet power, using a theory that came into general practice only following World War II. Bell was a pioneer in understanding that an engine can produce forward motion by emitting a jet of fluid or heated air and gases from its rear. Even though Bell faced many setbacks in this early research, he wrote in 1893 that "the more I experiment, the more convinced I become that flying machines are practical."

In 1896 Langley built the first successful unmanned heavier-than-air flying machine. In May of that year he invited Bell to his houseboat on the Potomac River in Quantico, Virginia. There Bell witnessed the first experiments with a steam-powered, propeller-driven flying machine. In 1907 Bell described the effect on his own interests of witnessing those trial runs:

> The sight of Langley's steam aerodrome circling in the sky convinced me that the age of the flying-machine was at hand. Encouraged and stimulated by this remarkable exhibition of success, I quietly continued my experiments in my Nova Scotia laboratory in the hope that I, too, might be able to contribute something of value to the world's knowledge of this important subject.

Langley had checked with a classics scholar about choosing the best word for a flying machine and was advised that it should be aerodrome, from the Greek words for "air" and "runner." Even though the rest of the world soon agreed on airplane, Bell clung to the other term out of loyalty to his friend. (Similarly, the father of the telephone refused to follow the common practice of saying "Hello" when answering the telephone, insisting instead on

"Hoy! Hoy!" Hoy, as the dictionary indicates, is an exclamation to attract attention.)

However quietly Bell may have been conducting his experiments, news of his preoccupation spread. In 1897 Bell met an important figure from his past: Sir William Thomson, whose fascination with the telephone at the Centennial Exhibition of 1876 had been so important to the then-young inventor. In 1892 Queen Victoria had honored Sir William by raising him to the peerage, or British nobility, and from that time on he was known as Lord Kelvin. Now the great British physicist, on a tour of America, met Bell in Halifax.

This time the two men did not see eye to eye. Mabel wrote her mother describing how Lord Kelvin had wasted no time in telling Bell how much he regretted Bell's interest in aeronautics. Later, in response to a letter from Mabel, Kelvin explained his behavior: "I wished to dissuade him from giving his valuable time and resources to attempts which I believed, and still believe, could only lead to disappointment, if carried on with any expectation of leading to a useful flying machine."

Lord Kelvin's concerns failed to deflect Bell from his current passion. Instead, with safety questions uppermost in his mind, Bell had been considering what route to follow in order to gain "practical experience of the conditions to be met with in the air" without risking human life. By June 1898 he had come to a conclusion. To Mabel, Bell wrote that "the importance of kite flying as a step to a practical flying machine grows upon me." With the goal of constructing a kite that would support the weight of a man and an engine, the laboratories at Beinn Bhreagh were soon turned over to this new industry.

Just as Bell's harmonic telegraph proved to be a dead end in itself but led to his invention of the telephone, so also Bell's kites played no important role in aviation history but led him nonetheless to a technological breakthrough.

Bell at work with his assistants on one of his tetrahedral kites.

After experimenting with huge kites of many different varieties, in late August 1902 Bell suddenly envisioned the shape that would not only serve his purpose in aeronautics but would also be useful in numerous other applications. In his notebook for August 25, 1902, Bell described a pyramidlike figure with three triangular sides and a triangular base. Such a solid figure with four triangular faces is called a tetrahedron. Bell said of this tetrahedral shape:

> I believe it will prove of importance not only in kite architecture—but in forming all sorts of skeleton framework for all sorts of constructing—a new method of architecture. May prove a substitute for arches—and bridge work generally. . . .Whole structures so solid and so perfectly braced by its construction that it may be treated as a solid body. . . . May be used . . . for . . . ceilings of large buildings &c. . . . All the parts can be made of metal—& made cheaply.

With this insight, Bell made another discovery for which the world was not quite ready. In years to come bridges and other structures would indeed be based on the tetrahedron, in what would come to be known as space-frame architecture. But when others, notably R. Buckminster Fuller, an American engineer, designer, and architect, discovered the importance of the tetrahedron and used their understanding of its structure to solve a variety of design problems from the late 1930s on, they would be unaware of Bell's previous work.

In December 1905, with no knowledge that his architectural innovation would not take the world by storm during his lifetime, Bell assembled 1,300 tetrahedral "cells" into a single kite. The kite was able to support a 165-pound man in a 10-mile breeze at a height of about 30 feet—and Bell took photographs to prove it. In the meantime, Mabel believed so strongly in the potential uses of the tetrahedral form that she took steps to ensure that Bell would not ignore the commercial applications of his work. She encouraged him to take out a patent, which was granted in September 1904. Then, when she discussed her husband's most recent discovery with engineers in Washington, D.C., they advised her to test tetrahedral construction before trying to establish a business based on it.

Casey Baldwin, a young engineer, came to the Bells' Nova Scotia home in 1906 to help Bell work with his tetrahedral structures. Baldwin stayed for the next 40 years, working on many different projects.

With the goal of finding a young, recently trained engineer to construct a tetrahedral structure, she wrote Douglas McCurdy, an engineering student at the University of Toronto who was the son of a close friend from Baddeck, to ask if he might have a friend interested in helping her husband with his current work. In this way Frederick W. Baldwin, known as Casey, found his way to the Bells' Nova Scotia home in the summer of 1906. Casey Baldwin, who held degrees in mechanical and electrical engineering, would end up making Beinn Bhreagh his home for more than 40 years.

The opening ceremony for Bell's tetrahedral tower, August 31, 1907. The tower failed to generate any commercial interest and was taken down shortly after Bell's death in 1922.

Mabel and Alec immediately took a liking to the young man, who was born in 1882 and was thus almost the same age as their two sons would have been. Baldwin began work on his first assignment, to build a tetrahedral tower on top of the Bells' mountain to show that it could hold up against the heavy winds that blew across the Bras d'Or Lakes. Mabel wrote her daughter Daisy in November 1906, "If only I had a third daughter, she should have this young fellow—but he seems to have no thought but tetrahedrons." Baldwin oversaw the construction of the tower, whose virtues included lightness, strength, rigidity, and easy assembly from mass-produced parts.

On August 31, 1907, Bell staged a formal opening ceremony to publicize the new form of architecture. His son-in-law Bert Grosvenor ran a spread on the tower in the *National Geographic Magazine,* and Baldwin published an article on it in *Scientific American.* But the tower generated no commercial interest, and 15 years later—during which time it required no repairs at all—Mabel had it taken down after her husband's death.

When Douglas McCurdy received his engineering degree in 1907, he returned to Baddeck, where he joined his friend Baldwin in Bell's employ. With the tower completed, they returned their attention to Bell's tetrahedron-based flying machine experiments. Two other young men joined them. Lieutenant Thomas E. Selfridge, a West Point graduate, knew of Bell's aeronautical research and foresaw the role aviation would come to play in the military. Bell arranged with President Theodore Roosevelt to have Selfridge sent to Beinn Bhreagh as an official observer for the U.S. Army. Then, in search of an engine expert, Bell also brought to Baddeck Glenn H. Curtiss, a bicycle mechanic and builder from Hammondsport, New York. Riding a motorcycle he had designed and manufactured himself, Curtiss had won the world's record for the fastest mile. In September 1907 Mabel suggested to Alec that he join the four young men in a formal research group along the lines of the Volta Associates of the 1880s. She had recently sold a piece of property and volunteered to put $20,000 toward the new association's expenses. (She later put up another $15,000 to extend the term of the association by six months.) And so on October 1, 1907, the Aerial Experiment Association (AEA) came into existence. According to the agreement the five men had drawn up,

> It has been thought advisable that the undersigned should work together as an association in which all have equal interest, the above-named gentlemen giving the benefit of their assistance in carrying out the ideas of the said Alexander Graham Bell, the said Alexander Graham Bell giving his assistance to these gentlemen in carrying out their own independent ideas relating to aerial locomotion, and all working together individually and conjointly in pursuance of their common aim "to get into the air" by the construction of a practical aerodrome driven by its own motive power and carrying a man. . . .

Before the AEA was dissolved, on March 31, 1909, it achieved several aviation firsts. On March 12, 1908, its first nontetrahedral machine, Selfridge's *Red Wing,* made the

Bell, center, with Glenn Curtiss, far left, and the other members of the Aerial Experiment Association.

first public flight in the United States, at Lake Keuka, New York. Although the Wrights had already flown many times, they had worked in secrecy and almost no one knew of their accomplishments until five years after their historic flight of December 17, 1903. Bell's AEA convinced a doubting public that rumors of manned flight were in fact true.

The AEA's second creation, Baldwin's *White Wing,* built in 1908, was the first flying machine in North America to use ailerons. Baldwin attached these hinged tips to the wings' edges, connecting them by wire to the pilot's seat so that he could tilt the wings up or down to correct the machine's balance when it leaned to either side.

On July 4, 1908, the third machine, Curtiss's *June Bug,* won a trophy sponsored by *Scientific American* for the first successful flight of a heavier-than-air machine flying a measured one-kilometer (0.62 mile) course. Bell himself was absent, but he expressed his delight in a telegram: "Hurrah for Curtiss! Hurrah for the *June Bug*! Hurrah for the Aerial Association!" Present to witness the *June Bug's* triumph were Bell's daughter Daisy and son-in-law David Fairchild. In his autobiography Fairchild wrote: "That brief afternoon . . . changed my vision of the world as it was to be. There was no longer the shadow of doubt in my mind that the sky would be full of aeroplanes and that the time would come when people would travel through the air faster and more safely than they did on the surface of the earth."

The AEA's fourth plane, McCurdy's *Silver Dart*, also achieved a first. On February 23, 1909, when McCurdy successfully flew it over the ice of Baddeck Bay, he became the first to fly a heavier-than-air machine in the British Empire.

Unfortunately, before the *Silver Dart* achieved its triumph, the AEA was also involved in a tragic aviation first when one of its members, Lieutenant Selfridge, became the first fatality in American aviation history. In August 1908 Selfridge was ordered back to Washington. Because of the knowledge he had acquired as a member of the AEA, the army assigned him to its recently formed Aeronautical Board. He felt honored to be chosen to accompany Orville Wright on a government-supported test flight at Fort Myer, Virginia. That flight, on September 17, 1908, ended in a crash that killed Selfridge and injured Wright.

By the terms of its agreement, the AEA disbanded at the end of March 1909. The Bells, however, urged McCurdy and Baldwin to continue its work. With the Bells' financial support, the two men formed the Canadian Aerodrome Company, with headquarters at Beinn Bhreagh. They hoped to interest the Canadian government in their machines, but interest never led to an actual order. The new company did, however, construct two flying machines, the *Baddeck No. 1* and *No. 2*.

Besides his early aeronautical experiments, his work with kites, and his involvement in the AEA, Bell helped advance aviation in North America in other ways. He seems never to have felt so competitive with the Wrights as to let their achievements make him jealous. Instead, as in his 1906 address to the Washington Academy of Sciences, he sang their praises: "Thanks to the efforts of the Wright brothers, the practicability of aerial flight by man is no longer problematical. . . . America may well feel proud of the fact that the problem has been first solved by citizens of the United States." Insisting that the Wrights' flights were extremely important, he paid for photographs to be made of them and gave the prints to the Smithsonian Institution. And using his influence as a regent of the Smithsonian, he persuaded the institution to establish a Langley Medal in support of aviation research.

Ultimately, however, Bell's reputation as an aviation pioneer never took root, much to Mabel's disappointment. In a letter of April 1919 to their son-in-law David Fairchild, Mabel lay the blame for this outcome on another member of the AEA, Glenn Curtiss. She compared him to those Johnnies-come-lately who had earlier tried to cheat Bell out of the fame he deserved for the telephone. But where those earlier attempts had proved unsuccessful, Curtiss had been all too successful:

> Curtiss, who knew every secret of the AEA, tried to find other methods [of designing airplanes] and failed utterly. He changed a few unessential details but his claim of having got around our principles had no more justification than would an assertion that putting the Bell Receiver in a slightly different holder made it no longer a Bell Receiver. Those biplanes [airplanes with two parallel sets of wings] you saw flying overhead and thought of as Curtiss biplanes are not really Curtiss biplanes at all, they are Baldwin biplanes constructed on AEA principles, just as [is] every other biplane now flying. The world does not know this—but Curtiss does, and it is due to him that the world does not.

Mabel went on to say that whereas Curtiss's only contribution to the AEA's work had been "the fitting of his motor," he had taken advantage of "my money, Mr. Bell's brains, and those of the other associates." She mused that if only Bell had had in his corner a man like her father, Gardiner Greene Hubbard, the situation might have been different. Without someone to promote him as an aviation pioneer with the same determination as Hubbard had promoted him as the inventor of the telephone, "Mr. Bell's name is rarely mentioned in connection with Aviation."

Did Bell share his wife's views on this matter? No confirmation has been found in the many written documents he left behind. Perhaps it is safe to assume that he took such delight in the aeronautical research itself that he felt no need for further fame.

A half-size model of Bell's tetrahedral triplane.

"I Want Many More Years of Life to Finish It All"

In the last year of his life, Bell lamented, "I cannot hope to work out half the problems in which I am interested." Indeed, a survey of just some of the experiments occupying Bell's time in his 60s and 70s shows an amazing variety of concerns.

Even while deeply involved in aeronautics, Bell had begun thinking about his next major line of experimentation. In his notes for September 2, 1901, he wrote:

> Whatever resistance the water may offer to a body going through it at a certain velocity—THE AIR WOULD OFFER LESS RESISTANCE. If, therefore, with increase of speed the boat or vessel could be elevated more and more out of the water so that the chief part of the resistance should be the air, would not the engine power be more economically utilised under such circumstances?

Bell's interest in aviation kept him focused on the problem. He began to think about airplanes taking off from water, and in 1906 he made his first sketch of a hydrofoil.

Bell's interest in aviation led him to develop the hydrofoil, shown here speeding across the surface of Bras D'Or Lake.

A hydrofoil is a boat that, when traveling at high speeds, can lift above the water's surface. The boat resembles an aircraft in that it has wings. But a hydrofoil's wings, or foils, are designed to move underwater. When a hydrofoil travels at low speed, it moves through the water on its shell, but at higher speeds the water rushes over the foils. As the pressure at the top of the foils drops, the foils rise in the water, causing the hydrofoil's hull to "fly" above the water. Because at high speeds a hydrofoil's frame does not have to be pushed through the water, it needs less power than other craft.

Bell was not the first person to conceive of hydrofoils, and he was aware of the work the Italian engineer and inventor Enrico Forlanini had been doing in the field. When Bell began work with Casey Baldwin on hydrofoil design in 1908, he hoped to make a contribution to what he considered "the most significant [invention] of recent years." In 1910–11, after the breakup of the AEA, the Bells and the Baldwins took a trip around the world. Although this delay put their experimental hydrofoil work on hold for a while, it enabled them to meet with Forlanini and take a ride on Lake Maggiore in his hydrofoil.

At the end of the trip Bell and Baldwin returned to their work at Beinn Bhreagh, hoping to design successful hydrofoils. Bell, now 64 years old, turned the management of the estate laboratories over to Baldwin but continued to work in what used to be the hangar, where his massive kites were stored.

Just as Bell insisted on using the word aerodrome for what was commonly called the airplane, he also insisted on calling hydrofoils hydrodromes, from the Greek for "water" and "runner." Bell and Baldwin referred to the Bell-Baldwin hydrofoils by the abbreviation HD. (According to Bell's last secretary, Catherine Mackenzie, during a particularly disappointing period of experimenta-

tion on the craft the joke circulated that HD really stood for "Hope Deferred.")

Between 1911 and the outbreak of World War II in August 1914, the Beinn Bhreagh labs turned out three HDs, all of which were disappointing, and an unsuccessful hydrofoil sailboat. Then, when the war broke out, Bell found himself in a dilemma. He was a citizen of the United States, which would not enter the war until April 6, 1917, but he spent much of his time in Canada, which entered the war immediately. Rather than violate his country's neutrality by working on seacraft whose potential military use was obvious, he converted the lab to the production of lifeboats for the Canadian navy.

Although Bell was firmly committed to world peace, he had no reservations about using his advances in technology to help his country. Two days after the United States entered the war, Bell returned from Washington to Beinn

Casey Baldwin (right) aboard one of the hydrofoils he designed with Bell.

Bhreagh. There he and Baldwin began work on an HD that they hoped would be of use against German submarines. They did not succeed—in part because the navy supplied the engines it had promised Bell only after the war had ended. Nevertheless, on September 9, 1919, less than a year after the war's end, their HD-4 set a world water-speed record of nearly 71 miles per hour. That record was not topped until 1963.

Following the war, Bell and Baldwin experienced mixed failure and success in what they hoped would be a new business to supply hydrofoils to the U.S. Navy or the British Admiralty. Official observers from both countries expressed admiration for the HDs, but neither government placed an order. Nonetheless, Bell was pleased when, on March 28, 1922, he and Baldwin received four U.S. patents related to their work in hydrofoils. As it happened, these were the last patents granted to Bell, who had recently turned 75. His original telephone patent had been granted almost exactly 46 years earlier.

Hydrofoils were by no means the only topic to engage Bell in his last years. As he told a reporter in December 1921, "There cannot be mental atrophy in any person who continues to observe, to remember what he observes, and to seek answers for his unceasing hows and whys about things." Among the issues that interested Bell in the last 10 years or so of his life were two that continue to occupy scientists in our own time: water and energy. The *National Geographic Magazine* for February 1917 printed a speech Bell delivered to the graduating class of a Washington, D.C., vocational school that month. He told the young people why these issues seemed so important to him and how he hoped to solve the problems they presented.

Bell explained that life in Cape Breton had made him acutely aware of the need to find ways to keep stranded fishermen from dying of thirst. Even though fishermen are surrounded by water, seawater is not, of course, fit to drink. To assist distressed seafarers, Bell devised an apparatus capable of removing the salt from seawater, thus rendering it drinkable. His inventive mind also came up with a way to turn a person's breath into drinking water. Since our breath contains water vapor, changing that vapor from a gas to a liquid—in other words, condensing it—should result in drinkable water. Cooling a vapor sufficiently causes it to condense. Bell described his offhand but clever approach to the problem:

> I took a bucket of cool salt water from the sea, put it down in the bottom of a boat between my knees, and then put into it a large empty bottle the size of a beer bottle, which floated in the water with the neck of the bottle resting on the edge of the bucket. Then I took a long glass tube, over a meter in length, and put one end into the bottle and the other end in my mouth. I sat back comfortably in a chair with the tube between my lips and inhaled through the nostrils and blew down through the tube. This process was so easily performed that I found I could read a book while it was going on.

According to Bell, he continued to breathe comfortably into the tube for more than two hours, at the end of which the bottle contained enough water to help quench thirst. When he tasted the water, he was a little dismayed by the taste, but as he concluded, "I don't suppose that would have mattered much to a man who was dying of thirst."

Even though Bell's comments about alternative energy sources and conserving and recycling energy date from 1917, the issues are timely enough to appear in today's press. At that early date Bell was focused on a problem that became a major world issue more than 50 years later. Before people began describing different energy sources as renewable or nonrenewable, Bell already had realized that what we now call fossil fuels take many millions of years to form: "We can take coal out of a mine," he said, "but we can

Bell developed a method for distilling water from exhaled human breath as a way to keep stranded fishermen from dying of thirst.

never put it back. We can draw oil from subterranean reservoirs, but we can never refill them again. We are spendthrifts in the matter of fuel and are using our capital for our running expenses."

Bell foresaw that the day would soon come when the world would run out of these fossil fuels, and he therefore proposed an alternative source of fuel: alcohol. He favored alcohol because it "makes a beautiful, clean, and efficient fuel" and can be made "from almost any vegetable matter capable of fermentation." Bell even had the idea, only now being put to use, of converting garbage into fuel.

A renewable form of energy that has found favor in recent years is solar power. Before solar panels appeared on a single roof in this country, Bell described the principle used in their design: "What wide expanses of roof are available in all our large cities for the utilization of the sun's rays! Simple pipes laid up on the roof and containing oil or some other liquid would soon become heated by the sun's rays. The hot oil could be carried into an insulated tank and stored."

Years before people had even begun to worry about buying the most energy-efficient appliances so as not to waste fuel, Bell was conscious of the need to conserve and recycle energy: "It is extraordinary how wasteful we are in our means of producing heat and in retaining it after it has been produced. It is safe to say that a great deal more heat goes up the chimney than we utilize from a fire."

Well before it became a common concern, Bell hoped to make constructive use of energy that was currently being lost. For example, he thought about ways in which he could employ the heat given off by a desk lamp. Shortly after Bell's death, George Kennan published an article about his friend in the weekly journal *The Outlook*. In it Kennan recalled Bell's work to conserve and recycle energy:

> At one time . . . his attention was drawn to the waste of heat that results from the burning of fuel in open fireplaces. He at once began a series of experiments to show how great this waste is and to prove that most of the lost heat might be conserved. One afternoon he took me up into the attic of his house to show me a wool-packed tank holding a hundred gallons or more of water whose temperature had been raised to 168 degrees by the conserved heat of an ordinary kerosene lamp burning in a room two or three stories below.

Though Bell's work on water and energy issues occupied much of his time in his final years, he nonetheless found time to play a role in telephone history once again. So did Tom Watson, his colleague of so many years earlier. On January 25, 1915, Bell in New York and Watson in San Francisco participated in the formal ceremonies dedicating the first telephone line to cross the North American continent. Among the other participants were President Woodrow Wilson and the governor of California. Before the transcontinental telephone line began to transmit ordinary conversation that January night, various dignitaries spoke to one another from different points across the country. From the White House, President Wilson, whom Bell admired greatly, congratulated the inventor for "this notable consummation of your long labors."

According to Bell's secretary, Catherine Mackenzie, an attempt was made to give Bell a prepared speech to read for the occasion, possibly to avoid embarrassing him, because his hearing had begun to decline. Bell refused to follow anyone else's script, however, so this conversation between the two former coworkers was nearly as spontaneous as their first one had been 39 years earlier. This time, instead of being in two different rooms in the same Boston rooming house, Bell was on the East Coast, Watson on the West. Characteristically, Bell began this conversation with Watson not with "Hello" but with his almost trademarked "Hoy, Hoy." He went on to pay tribute to the "many, many minds" who had transformed his invention into the modern telephone service.

The high point of the conversation was yet to come, however. Watson described his reaction to it in his autobiography:

> Dr. Bell asked me to wait a moment until he could connect another transmitter through which he wanted to talk with me. I waited, and in a few moments his voice came over the wire as loudly and distinctly as before, saying: "I am now talking through a duplicate of the first telephone you made for me and that we tested together in June, 1875. Do you hear me?" I answered that I heard him perfectly. Then, when he repeated to me the famous first sentence, "Mr. Watson, come here, I want you," and I answered, "I should be very glad to, Dr. Bell, but we are now so far apart it would take me a week to come instead

of a minute," it seemed to me as if forty years of telephone achievement had been condensed into a thrilling moment.

By 1915 partial loss of his hearing was not the only sign that Bell's health had begun to decline. He had also been diagnosed as suffering from diabetes, a disease in which the body cannot use sugar normally. Although there is still no cure for diabetes, many diabetics today receive injections of insulin, a hormone that regulates the body's use of sugar and other food. Insulin was not, however, used to treat diabetic patients until 1922. When Bell developed diabetes, the only treatment for the disease was control of the diet. Bell was far from a model patient, however, from time to time eating whatever he wanted. For example, if he picked up his grandson Melville at school, he would often suggest that they stop at a bakery on the way home, where he not only treated the boy to a sugary snack but also indulged in one himself.

Bell at work with his longtime secretary, Catherine Mackenzie, in 1919, three years before his death.

Despite his diabetes, Bell maintained quite an active schedule, which included lecturing and traveling in addition to conducting his experiments. In the fall of 1920 he returned to his native Scotland for the last time. Edinburgh, where he had been a mediocre student, now welcomed him as a distinguished native son. His former school celebrated his return by giving a half holiday to the current students, who celebrated the news by greeting the "old boy" with a roar of appreciation. Bell also visited Elgin, where he had been a teacher himself so many years before and where he had begun the experiments with vowel sounds that had ultimately led to the telephone.

Bell traveled again during the winter of 1921–22, this time in Florida and the Caribbean. Never one to take a true vacation, Bell continued his work while he traveled. In late February 1922, just short of his 75th birthday, he was visiting his daughter Daisy and her husband David in their Florida home. From there he wrote his other son-in-law, Bert Grosvenor, of his work on a process to purify water, which he hoped to patent. There were signs, however, that his strength was diminishing. A cruise he was taking stopped in Venezuela, where Bell was invited to visit the Caracas school for the deaf, but he felt too tired to go. In Jamaica, though, he spent a hot day driving by himself, looking unsuccessfully for the grave of a seafaring relative who had died there more than a century earlier.

Bell's doctors gave him a thorough checkup on his return to Washington but found no striking change in his health. With their blessing he returned to Beinn Bhreagh. There he resumed work so vigorously that Mabel saw no reason to urge Elsie and Bert Grosvenor to change their plans for a summer trip to South America.

One day at the end of July, Bell made extensive observations in what he called Sheepville, then spent most of the night reading, as was his habit. But when Daisy and David

Fairchild arrived at Beinn Bhreagh on July 30, a few days earlier than expected, they learned that Bell had not been able to get up since his return from Sheepville and that he had no appetite. Then he seemed a little stronger on August 1 and asked his secretary to take down what he had to say. As he spoke, someone said, "Don't hurry." Bell answered, "I have to."

David Fairchild spent that night by his father-in-law's side. Just before 2:00 A.M. on August 2, 1922, Fairchild summoned Mabel. As she spoke his name, he opened his eyes and smiled at her. He died shortly thereafter. Later that day, Mabel sent a telegram to the Grosvenors: "Father died peacefully today. Only within a few days did we realize any danger."

With great dignity and personal flair, Mabel managed the details of Bell's simple funeral, which was held on

Bell was buried on August 4, 1922. All telephone service in the United States was stopped for one minute as a tribute to the man who had invented the telephone.

August 4. Having recalled a chance remark of her husband's years earlier that he would like to be buried at the top of their "Beautiful Mountain," she arranged for the body to be lowered into a grave site blasted out of rock beneath Casey Baldwin's tetrahedral tower. Bell's laboratory workers built his coffin out of local pine and lined it with fabric left over from the days of the huge kites.

Mabel told the mourners not to wear black, a color her husband had never liked. In a letter to Elsie on August 6, Daisy explained her mother's decision not to wear mourning garb and not to have the others wear it: "She says she could never take it off if she did, [and] she couldn't help watching us for the first signs of our putting it off. It would seem like putting off our sorrow."

At 6:25 P.M., on August 4, 1922, to coincide with the burial of the inventor of the telephone, all telephone service in the United States was suspended for a full minute.

On another August day 46 years earlier, Mabel Hubbard had written a letter to her fiancé, Alec Bell, who was spending some time with his parents at their home in Brantford, Ontario. She described a conversation she had had with her mother in which they were worried about their hopes for Alec's future. In the letter Mabel conveyed her concerns that Alec would never accomplish anything if he continued to be interested in everything. She urged him to "make yours a useful life for the benefit of those around you and the world at large."

Despite the fact that Alexander Graham Bell's mind continued to be "drawn off to every new idea that comes up," Mabel's husband did in fact lead a life that benefited countless others. After his death, colleagues, rivals, and friends alike commented on the extent of Bell's contributions to society. On August 15, 1922, the directors of the American Telephone and Telegraph Company entered into their minutes this comment: "In the invention of the telephone he founded the art of transmitting speech electrically, a new and invaluable contribution to the humanizing of mankind." Even Bell's former rival Thomas Edison referred to the social significance of Bell's invention of the telephone: "My late friend, Alexander Graham Bell, whose world-famed invention annihilated time and space, brought the human family in closer touch."

Bell's contributions to humanity went well beyond his invention of the telephone, however, as George Kennan noted in an article published several weeks after Bell's death: "His work in many fields added greatly to human happiness and left a permanent impress on the world."

On a plaque near the foyer of the Alexander Graham Bell Museum at Baddeck, Nova Scotia, visitors can read the following statement: "The inventor is a man who looks upon the world and is not contented with things as they are. He wants to improve whatever he sees, he wants to benefit the world. . . ." These words are taken from a speech Bell delivered to the Patent Congress of 1891 in Washington, D.C. How fitting, then, that Bell's gravestone proudly bears the word inventor.

March 3, 1847
Alexander Graham Bell is born in Edinburgh, Scotland.

Fall 1865
Bell begins his first serious work on the science of speech production while a teacher at Weston House Academy in Elgin, Scotland.

August 1870
Bell emigrates to Canada with parents.

April 1871
He begins his career as teacher of the deaf in the United States.

Fall 1871
He begins his appointment as professor of vocal physiology at Boston University's School of Oratory.

February 27, 1875
Bell, with Gardiner Greene Hubbard and Thomas Sanders, forms what came to be known as the Bell Patent Association.

March 1–2, 1875
Bell meets with Joseph Henry, secretary of the Smithsonian Institution, who encourages him to continue his work on the telephone.

June 2, 1875
Bell generates the first sound-shaped electric current, while working with Thomas Watson on a harmonic telegraph.

June 25, 1876
He demonstrates the telephone at the Centennial Exhibition in Philadelphia and is later awarded a prize over the signature of Sir William Thomson, the noted British physicist.

Bell on the steps of the Volta Bureau with the members of the Executive Committee of the American Association for the Promotion of the Teaching of Speech to the Deaf.

July 9, 1877
Bell forms the Bell Telephone Company with Gardiner Greene Hubbard, Thomas Sanders, and Thomas Watson.

July 11, 1877
Bell marries Mabel Hubbard.

May 8, 1878
Daughter Elsie is born.

February 15, 1880
Daughter Marian (Daisy) is born.

1878–97
Bell defends his claim to the telephone patent in more than 600 legal cases and wins each one.

1881
He establishes the Volta Laboratory in Washington, D.C., with money from the French government's Volta Prize, given in 1880 for his invention of the telephone.

1882
Alexander Graham Bell becomes a United States citizen.

1883
Bell begins publication of *Science* magazine. Elected to the National Academy of Sciences.

1886
He establishes the Volta Bureau as a center for studies on the deaf, with his share of money from the sale of Volta Laboratory associates' patents going towards improvements to the phonograph.

1898
Bell is elected President of the National Geographic Society and serves in this position until 1903.

October 1, 1907
With funding from Mabel H. Bell, he forms the Aerial Experiment Association with F. W. ("Casey") Baldwin, Douglas McCurdy, Thomas E. Selfridge, and Glenn H. Curtiss.

January 25, 1915
Bell participates in formal ceremonies dedicating the first transcontinental telephone line.

March 28, 1922
With "Casey" Baldwin, Bell receives four patents covering their work on hydrofoils.

August 2, 1922
Alexander Graham Bell dies at his estate, Beinn Bhreagh, in Baddeck, Nova Scotia.

Bell's Nova Scotia estate, Beinn Bhreagh.

FURTHER READING

Biographies

Bruce, Robert V. Bell: *Alexander Graham Bell and the Conquest of Solitude.* Boston: Little, Brown, 1973.

Burlingame, Roger. *Out of Silence Into Sound: The Life of Alexander Graham Bell.* New York: Macmillan, 1964.

Costain, Thomas B. *The Chord of Steel: The Story of the Invention of the Telephone.* New York: Doubleday, 1960.

Davidson, Margaret. *The Story of Alexander Graham Bell, Inventor of the Telephone.* New York: Dell, 1989.

Eber, Dorothy Harley. *Genius at Work: Images of Alexander Graham Bell.* New York: Viking, 1982.

Mackenzie, Catherine D. *Alexander Graham Bell: The Man Who Contracted Space.* Boston: Houghton Mifflin, 1928. Biography by his personal assistant.

St. George, Judith. *Dear Dr. Bell—Your Friend, Helen Keller.* New York: Putnam, 1992.

Toward, Lilias M. *Mabel Bell, Alexander's Silent Partner.* New York: Methuen, 1984.

Autobiographies of People Associated with Bell

Fairchild, David. *The World Was My Garden: Travels of a Plant Explorer.* New York: Scribners, 1943.

Keller, Helen. *The Story of My Life.* Garden City, N.Y.: Doubleday, 1904.

Watson, Thomas A. *Exploring Life: The Autobiography of Thomas A. Watson.* New York: Appleton, 1926.

Articles by Bell in *National Geographic Magazine*

"Aerial Locomotion: With a Few Notes of Progress in the Construction of an Aerodrome." (January 1907): 1–34.

"Discovery and Invention." (June 1914): 649–55.

"The National Geographic Society." (March 1912): 272–98.

"Our Heterogeneous System of Weights and Measures: An Explanation of the Reasons Why the United States Should Abandon Its Obsolete System of Inches, Tons, and Gallons." (March 1906): 158–69.

"Prehistoric Telephone Days." (March 1922): 223–41.

"Prizes for the Inventor: Some of the Problems Awaiting Solution." (February 1917): 131–46.

"The Tetrahedral Principle in Kite Structure." (June 1903): 219–51.

"Who Shall Inherit Long Life? On the Existence of a Natural Process at Work Among Human Beings Tending to Improve the Vigor and Vitality of Succeeding Generations." (June 1919): 505–14.

Articles about Bell in *National Geographic Magazine*

Bruce, Robert V. "Alexander Graham Bell." (September 1988): 358–85.

Grosvenor, Gilbert M. "Canada's Winged Victory, The *Silver Dart*: Canadians Re-enact Their Historic First Flight of Half a Century Ago." (August 1959): 254–67.

———. "Dr. Bell's Tetrahedral Tower." (October 1907): 672–75.

Lesage, Jean. "Alexander Graham Bell Museum: Tribute to Genius." (August 1956): 227–56.

Other Books and Articles about Bell, His Achievements, and His Colleagues

Baida, Peter. "Breaking the Connection: The Story of AT&T . . ." *American Heritage* (June–July 1985): 65ff.

Barnett, Lincoln. "The Voice Heard Round the World." *American Heritage* (April 1965): 50ff.

The Bell Telephone: The Deposition of Alexander Graham Bell in the Suit Brought by the United States to Annul the Bell Patents. Boston: American Bell Telephone, 1908.

Benz, Francis E. *Talking Round the Earth: The Story of the Telephone.* New York: Dodd, Mead, 1942.

Boettinger, H. M. *The Telephone Book: Bell, Watson, Vail and American Life: 1876–1976.* Croton-on-Hudson, N.Y.: Riverwood, 1977.

Boyne, Walter J. *The Smithsonian Book of Flight for Young People.* New York: Atheneum, 1988.

Brooks, John. *Telephone: The First Hundred Years.* New York: Harper & Row, 1976.

Grosvenor, Lilian. "My Grandfather Bell." *New Yorker* (November 11, 1950): 44–48.

Kennan, George. "A Few Recollections of Alexander Graham Bell." *Outlook* (September 27, 1922): 146–49.

Lash, Joseph P. *Helen and Teacher: The Story of Helen Keller and Anne Sullivan Macy.* New York: Delacorte, 1980.

Parkin, John Hamilton. *Bell and Baldwin, Their Development of Aerodromes and Hydrodromes at Baddeck, Nova Scotia.* Toronto: University of Toronto Press, 1964.

Ryder, John D., and Donald G. Fink. *Engineers and Electrons: A Century of Electrical Progress.* New York: Institute of Electrical and Electronics Engineers, 1984.

Sharlin, Harold I. *The Making of the Electrical Age: From the Telegraph to Automation.* New York: Abelard-Schuman, 1964.

Winefield, Richard. *Never the Twain Shall Meet: Bell, Gallaudet, and the Communications Debate.* Washington, D.C.: Gallaudet University Press, 1987.

Page numbers in *italics* indicate illustrations.

Aerial Experiment Association, 113, *114*, 115-16
Alexander Graham Bell Association for the Deaf, 100
Alexander Graham Bell School, 93
American Academy of Arts and Sciences, 53, 106
American Association for the Advancement of Science, 82
American Association for the Promotion of the Teaching of Speech to the Deaf, 96, 97, 99
American Convention of Instructors of the Deaf, 95-97
American Foundation for the Blind, 102
American Telephone and Telegraph Company, 130
Arthur, Chester, 74
Audiometer, 93-94

Baldwin, Frederick "Casey," *111*-13, 114, 120-22
Bell, Alexander (grandfather), 11, 13, 15-16, 17
Bell, Alexander Graham
ancestry, 11, 13
death of, 127-30
development of telephone, 10-11, 20, 36-39, 45-47, 50-55, 56, 59
early scientific work, 18-19, 23

early years, 13-18
education, 14-15
visits England, 61-64
fiber optics and, 84-86
financial problems, 48
dispute with Edward Gallaudet, 94-98
and harmonic telegraph, 9-10, 29, 33, 42-45, 48
designs hydrofoil, 118, 120-22
influence of grandfather, 16
laboratories of, 76, 78-80
studies longevity, 101
medical inventions, 71-74
moves to Canada, 23
opposes sign language, 94-95
as patron of science, 81-83, 87, 89
improves phonograph, 78-79
as pioneer of aviation, 105-11, 113-17
and recycling of energy, 122-25
understanding of sound, 30-32
invention of telephone challenged, 64-69, 70-71
devises tetrahedron, 110-13
and Thomas Watson, 43-44
wins Volta Prize, 78
works with deaf, 19, 23, 24-28, 64, 79, 91-103
Bell, Alexander Melville (father), *11*, 13, 15, 16-17, 18, 19, 23, 39
Bell, Chichester (cousin), 78, 79

Bell, Daisy (daughter), 89, 93, 112, 115, 128
Bell, David (uncle), 13
Bell, Edward (brother), 11, *15*, 19
Bell, Edward (son), 73-75
Bell, Eliza Grace Symonds (mother), 11, 13-14, 19
Bell, Elsie (daughter), 73, 83, 93
Bell, Mabel Hubbard (wife), 26-27, 33-35, *34*, 48, 58-59, 64, 66, 68, 75, 79-80, 87, 92, 93, 97, 101, 106, 107, 109, 111, 116, 129-30
Bell, Marian (daughter), 73
Bell, Melville (brother), 11, *15*, 19
Bell Patent Association, 43, 55
Bell, Robert (son), 75
Bell Telephone Company, 66-69, 106
Beinn Bhreagh, 80, 100-101, 111, 120, 127-30, *135*
Blake, Clarence J., 36, 39, 68
Boston University, 33-34

Canadian Aerodrome Company, 115
Clarke School for the Deaf, 26, 40
Curtiss, Glenn H., 113-17

Decibels, 32
Dolbear, Amos E., 30
Dom Pedro II, emperor of Brazil, 54-55
Edison, Thomas, 56, 65-66, 78, 131
Einstein, Albert, 82

Electric motor, 21-22
Electromagnet, 20-21
Electromagnetism, 20-22
Ellis, Alexander, 18

Fairchild, David, 89, 115, 116, 128-29
Faraday, Michael, 22
Fiber optics, 84-86
Field, Kate, 61, 68
Forlanini, Enrico, 120
Fuller, R. Buckminster, 111

Gallaudet, Edward, *94*-98, 99
Garfield, James, 71-73, *74*
Government Case, 70-71, 93
Gray, Elisha, 30, 50-51, 54, 64-66, *67*, 69, 70
Grosvenor, Gilbert, 83, 87, 89, 128

Harmonic telegraph, 9, 29, 33, 42-45, 48
Hearing, explained, 31-32
Helmholtz, Hermann von, 18, 28, 36
Henry, Joseph, 9-11, 20-22, 45
Hubbard, Gardiner Greene, 26-27, 40, 42-*43*, 44, 47-48, 50, 53-54, 55, 65, 66-67, 82
Hubbard, Mabel. *See* Bell, Mabel Hubbard
Hydrofoil, 118, *119*, 120-22

Induction balance, 72-73

Johnson, William, 26

Keller, Helen, 101-*3*
Kennan, George, 87, 89, 125

Langley, Samuel P., 82, *107*-9

Mackenzie, Catherine, 71, 120-21, 126, *129*
Massachusetts Institute of Technology, 28, 36, 53

McCurdy, Douglas, 111, 113, 115
"Memoir upon the Formation of a Deaf Variety of the Human Race" (Bell), 99
Metal vacuum jacket, *74*
Michelson, Albert A., 81-82, *84*
Mohawk Indians, 26
Monroe, Lewis, 28, 33, 47
Morley, Edward, 81
Morse, Samuel F. B., 42
Mr. Bell's Primary School, 92-93

National Academy of Sciences, 75, 98, 107, 116
National Geographic Magazine, 83, 87, *88*, 112, 122
Nature, 82

Oersted, Hans Christian, 20
Oxford University, 64

Pan-Electric Company, 70
Peary, Robert, 105
Perkins School for the Blind, 101-2
Photophone, *84*-85

Reis, Philip, 70
Rogers, Harry, 70

Sanders, George, 27-28, 33, 42-43, 48, 101
Sanders, Thomas, 27-28, 42-43, 44, 48, 50, 66
Science, 82
Scientific American, 112, 114
Selfridge, Thomas E., 113, 114, 115
Sign language, 94-95
Smithsonian Astrophysical Observatory, 82
Smithsonian Institution, 9, 83, 107, 116
Sound waves, 30-32
measured, 32
Standard Elocutionist, The (Bell), 13

Story of My Life, The (Keller), 102
Sullivan, Anne, 101-2, *103*
Sympathetic vibration, 30-31

Tainter, Charles Sumner, 78, *79*, 84-85
Telegraph, 29, 33, 42-43
Telephone, 9-10, 36-39, 45-47, 50-55, 59
basic principles of, 20-22, 56-57
demonstrated by Bell, 58-59, 61-63
dispute over invention of, 64-69, 70-71
See also Electromagnetism
Telephone probe, 73
Thompson, Charles, 71
Thomson, William (Lord Kelvin), 54-55, 109

Visible Speech, *12*, 13, 19, 23, 24, 26, 27-28, 34, 36, 48, 53, 54, 64, 93
Visible Speech Pioneer, The, 28
Volta, Alessandro, 78
Volta Associates, 113
Volta Bureau, 79, 99
Volta Laboratory, 78-79
Volta Prize, 78

Watson, Thomas A., 43-44, *45*-47, 51-53, 55, 56, 58-59, 65, 66-69, 70, 78, 105-6, 125-27
Western Union Telegraph Company, 29, 42, 55, 65, 66, 69
Weston House Academy, 17
Wilson, Woodrow, 125-26
Wright, Orville, 105, 114, 115
Wright, Wilbur, 105, 114

ACKNOWLEDGMENTS

I wish to take this opportunity to express my thanks to a number of people who generously assisted me in preparing this book. John Rutter, Permissions Coordinator of the National Geographic Society, kindly granted me permission to quote directly from Bell's articles in the Society's magazine. Also at National Geographic, William Allen was my liaison with the staff, and Carrie Westenberg provided useful information.

Two librarians were especially helpful. At Boston University, Margaret Goostray gave me access to the Bell materials in the Special Collections of the university library. Donna Meehan, librarian at the Clarke School for the Deaf, sent me bound copies of four lectures given from 1974 to 1977 in the Alexander Graham Bell Lecture Series begun by the school's trustees "to recognize significant work done in the field of deafness and related areas," along with other material.

Keith Waters at the DEC Cambridge Research Lab was kind enough to demonstrate computer-based work that relates to Melville Bell's Visible Speech. Although Dr. Waters was unaware of Melville Bell's earlier work, he and other computer scientists at Digital Equipment Corporation have devised their own table of Visible Speech, based on an observation of real lips. His work is aimed at improving the synthetic speech produced by computers.

At the Smithsonian Institution, two scientists in the Division of Electricity at the National Museum of American History generously found the time to read all or parts of a draft of the book. Dr. Bernard Finn and Elliot Sivowitch helped me refine my descriptions of the early Bell telephones and other related technology. At Williams College, Susan Kaufman cheerfully spent hours in the library on my behalf, making copies of Bell's articles.

I am greatly obliged to Professor Owen Gingerich of Harvard University and to Nancy Toff of Oxford University Press for inviting me to participate in this series and for their comments. Although I have written a variety of books on a variety of subjects, high on my list of those that have given me the greatest pleasure are my biographies of Marie Curie and of Alexander Graham Bell.

Of course, I take full responsibility for the contents of this book, and none of the aforementioned helpful individuals should be held responsible for any errors that may remain in it.

Finally, and foremost, I wish to express my gratitude to my husband and to my daughters, who not only graciously listened to Alexander Graham Bell trivia during the months of research but who also read and made insightful comments on the draft manuscript. Their encouragement, willingness to help, and patience with me whatever my mood mean more to me than I can say.

Naomi Pasachoff, a research associate at Williams College, is the coauthor of several school and college science textbooks and author of a variety of other textbooks and trade books, including *Marie Curie and the Science of Radioactivity* in the *Oxford Portraits in Science* series. She has taught English composition and literature at Williams College, Rensselaer Polytechnic Institute, and Skidmore College. She holds an A.B. from Radcliffe College, Harvard University, an A.M. from Columbia University, and a Ph.D. from Brandeis University.

Owen Gingerich is Professor of Astronomy and of the History of Science at the Harvard-Smithsonian Center for Astrophysics in Cambridge, Massachusetts. The author of more than 400 articles and reviews, he has also written *The Great Copernicus Chase and Other Adventures in Astronomical History* and *The Eye of Heaven: Ptolemy, Copernicus, Kepler.*